Erasable

A Sacred Journey
of Invisibility to Clarity

Millie America

Powerful You!
PUBLISHING
Sharing Wisdom ~ Shining Light

Erasable

A Sacred Journey of Invisibility to Clarity

Copyright © 2023

The intent of the author is to provide general information to individuals who are taking positive steps in their lives for emotional and spiritual well-being. If you use any of the information in this book for yourself, the author and the publisher assume no responsibility for your actions. Readers are encouraged to seek the counsel of competent professionals with regards to such matters.

Powerful You! Publishing is committed to publishing works of quality and integrity. In that spirit, we are proud to offer this book to our readers; however, the story, the experiences, and the words are the author's alone.

Published by: Powerful You! Inc. USA
powerfulyoupublishing.com

Library of Congress Control Number: 2022923448

Millie America – First Edition

ISBN: 978-1-959348-07-8

First Edition January 2023

BIOGRAPHY & AUTOBIOGRAPHY / Women

ACKNOWLEDGEMENTS & GRATITUDE

I have a massive tribe of friends and family who have supported me in the creation and telling of this story. I thank you all from the bottom of my heart. It would take pages for me to point out every single one of you. The list grows daily. You know who you are and I adore you.

To my children, Nelson, Patrick, Valerica, Tunde, Bryan, Angelica, Kali, and Luke: There would be no story without you all in it. You have made me a mother, a more compassionate human, and a student of love. Thank you for the love, support, and presence in my life. I am forever touched that you all picked me as a mama. I believe the reason I am here is to be on this journey of awesomeness with each of you, near or afar. You are in my thoughts and prayers every single day.

To my beautiful stepchildren, Mark and Paul: You are always in my heart. Your parents have done such an amazing job with you both. Mary, I am forever grateful for the love and friendship we share after so much growth and heartache. Your endless compassion and forgiveness have changed me. I am in love with you…forever. Thank you for your infinite love with my children.

To A.H.: No habría historia de crecimiento y perdón sin ti. Soy la persona en la que me he convertido en gran parte debido a nuestra historia. Gracias por las increíbles lecciones. Te amaré para siempre, por todo lo que haces por cada uno de nuestros hijos. Y, en los últimos años, por extender tu generoso corazón hacia mí y tus nietos. Esta vida es mas rica por tu presencia.

To my parents: Your passion created me. Your journeys molded me. I am grateful to have picked you as parents. I cannot imagine a life without your powerful love. I have learned from your experiences and choices what to be and who not to become. However, at times, genetics plays an intricate role in our decisions. I felt love and this is the most important element to our story.

To M.P.: Our story taught me more about myself than any other relationship. I cannot thank you enough for the union because I will never be the same again. I have grown and healed because of our story. I am forever grateful for all those years. You have been an intricate character in my journey to self-love and acceptance.

To Sue Urda and Kathy Fyler, thank you for trusting in me and helping birth this book. And, to the incredible editor, Dana Micheli, you had your work cut out for you! You were a lifeline to what was written and what has evolved. All three of you have given me the courage to share this memoir through love and support. I am beyond grateful for the incredible journey with you three.

A special thanks to my friend, Sophia Phillips, for the beautiful author's photo she took of me. She's incredibly talented. You can find her at sophiasperspective.com

A NOTE FROM THE AUTHOR

As all stories, I've done my best to retell and share things as accurately as possible. I wrote the first part of this book twenty years ago, right after the accident. Those conversations, I consider, pretty accurate. And, whatever I haven't captured in pure perfection, I have expressed the essence of the conversations. I have changed names of people to respect their privacy.

I am well aware that stories are written from the level of perception and experiences. May this book help you understand that you are created to be seen. You are created through love for love. I pray you never ever doubt the exquisite light you carry in this world. I love you.

TABLE OF CONTENTS

FOREWORD

Have you ever met someone and knew that everything in your life was about to change because of it? This is my experience with Millie America. Well, excuse me, that's actually *Miss* America to you.

Millie and I were connected through an online group we were both a part of, organized by mutual friends. We met fairly regularly, and although this group provided amazing conversation between like-minded ladies I didn't really get to know Millie and the others very well. One day I reached out and asked if we could connect; she immediately said she would love that.

At that time, I was in what I called the "walking phase" of my life. I was in Colorado, after all, and getting up silly early in the morning and doing outdoor activities, regardless of the weather, is a natural part of the extreme sport lifestyle. I was walking upwards of eight miles a day. I would use part of that time as quiet meditation, or to listen to podcasts, have meetings with people all over the world, and catch up with friends and family. In hindsight, I understand that I was deeply depressed, and I was seeking connection and comfort, and this really helped me. It was easy to schedule a talk with Millie during these walks. She was on the East Coast (two time zones ahead of mine) and had two young children, so she was up long before I was. My intention was to have a "get to know each other call," however, what happened was far richer.

Although my memory is not always the best, I can recall almost every detail of that call. She was so easy to talk to and HILARIOUS, and my spirits were immediately lifted. She is also an extraordinarily gifted medium, so after some basic chitchat (I asked about the children, not really understanding that she had eight of them, including two grandchildren she had adopted), she couldn't help herself but to start giving me a reading.

Though I have had many psychics in my life, I didn't know any mediums personally. This was not something I had ever sought out, even though my sister and I are the last of our lineages on both sides of the family. Also, I had been in Colorado for more than twenty years, yet no one in my friend group there had ever met my dad, who died in 1996, and only a handful had met my mom, who passed in 2016.

A couple of minutes into this delightful conversation—and from what seemed like out of nowhere—Millie said, "Your dad loves his meat." This literally stopped me mid-stride.

"I am sorry, what did you say?"

"I said..."Millie repeated, "Your father, he loves to eat meat, he loves it!"

I immediately started to cry, almost uncontrollably, because how on earth does this woman know my father loved meat?! She went on to describe his spirit, his laugh, his big personality, and his heart. She told me he was with me all the time and is so proud of me. This was entirely overwhelming and even makes me cry as I am writing this. I had no idea how much I needed to hear those words from my father, and it was clear that he was actually speaking *through* her.

What no one in my current life knew was that my father and grandfather started a wholesale meat business the year I was born and my father LOVED meat. We had A LOT of it when I was growing up! In fact, to the contrary, today most people know me as a vegetarian or, on rare occasion, a pescatarian— a fact that my mother and sister insisted made Dad roll over in his grave!

Millie went on to give me a reading that literally changed my life and got me out of the depression I was in. There aren't enough words to express my gratitude and appreciation for that day and soooo many more since.

When Millie asked me to read the draft of *Erasable*, I was totally honored to be asked. (I mean, seriously, me???) I cuddled up with my Chromebook and read the whole thing in one day. I was and I am totally moved by her words and experiences. Let's be clear, I know I am biased, however, reading about my friend in this light taught me about perseverance and resilience in a deeply profound way. Millie's writing has a way of taking you to another dimension, her dimension, where someone could maneuver and make it through a life that was nearly erased by police, doctors, those that loved her, and even her own brain.

Erasable is a must-read, especially if you are needing a touch of perspective and a massive dose of irrepressible strength to get through obstacles in your own life.

As a side note, as I am a vegetarian my father has chosen to consult with Millie from time to time as she grocery shops for meat.

AND the most important thing (IF you are ever asked) is, I LOVE MILLIE MOST ;-)

Rebecca Saltman
www.disruptforgood.life

Part 1
The Mind

"Biology gives you a brain.
Life turns it into a mind."
~ Jeffrey Eugenides ~

CHAPTER 1

I wake up cold. It's night. I rise from the pavement feeling extra weight, and I know it's not mine. But it is. There is heaviness on my head that feels like I am drunk. Drunk like I've never felt before. I rise to darkness, and then to light as my eyes begin to focus. Looking down, I see bloodstains on my Bermuda shorts, the thick blood on my scraped knees, and that's when the pain comes. I touch the back of my head and feel a large bump that pushes from the inside out. It is about the size of a lemon, and tender, and when I press on it the pain burns into my eyes and into my brain. I sit back on the floor, shivering, though it is not a cold night. I caress my forehead and notice dry blood on my palms. I touch another bump that feels like a horn pushing from inside my forehead. The tops of my eyebrows are full of dirt. My cheeks are sandy. I wipe the dirt off with my shirt. I try to get up again, but it feels better to sit on the pavement. I see lights, and I know where I am—the park near our apartment, though for some reason it seems bigger and nicer than usual. I am cold and cannot stop my lips from shaking. That's when I notice that I am wearing an oversized t-shirt I don't remember seeing before. I can't read what it says. I can't focus on it. Fighting waves of dizziness, I pull myself up and gather my flip flops, but when I try to place them on my feet I fall to the ground once more. I have to finish dinner. I have to be home before him. I rush to move, but I can't. Everything will have to wait.

The park is half-lit, and I can't find the exit. I am feeling pressure from the inside of my head. I can't remember how I got here. This is *not*, I realize, the same park near our home. I make it out to a street. It is not my street. Cars seem strange. They are smaller, more compact. I am alone and numbed, iced to the core of my outer layers. I am alone in confusion. I am disoriented and I can't figure out which way to turn. I pick the left.

I walk for what feels like miles, and though I'm lost and dazed I try, unsuccessfully, to come up with an explanation as to where I've been. And all the while, the questions race through my mind.

How will I explain this to him? Did I leave dinner on the table? Where exactly is the apartment? What park was that? Why can't I remember? I am lost and cold and alone. Will that be a sufficient excuse?

I begin to cry. Everything seems unfocused in this darkness. I walk on a straight sidewalk along a large lake. I can hear the sounds of crickets, frogs, and other creatures that scare me even more. Are there alligators in that lake? I think I hear their sounds. My heart races at the thought of one coming out to eat me.

My breathing is heavy, my mind is lost, and my head is still carrying that extra weight. It is heavy and foggy and chilly, just like the rest of my body. I am shivering. I am on the border of hysteria, thinking I will never find my way back to where the fuck I'm supposed to go. A jogger passes by me, and I beg for his help. He pulls his hood over his head and keeps running.

Exhaustion seeps through every inch of me, yet I push on, searching desperately for something familiar. I pass a school, but can't read the name. I turn onto the street parallel to it and walk without an agenda through several different communities of large new houses. I walk past more lakes. I walk thinking about alligators and the frogs. The coldness of the night engulfs me, and everything begins to shake like the wind passing through the trees.

Again, my thoughts turn to my husband. He is going to be worried. Did he get his dinner? Did he get all he wanted tonight before I left? When did I leave? Did I leave before or after he made it home from work? I want to be cuddled up in his arms in our bed, not wandering, lost and alone through this strange place. It is very different from the worn-down neighborhood where we live. This place is new, and full of lakes, palm trees, new sidewalks, and creatures I don't want to know about. I sob, crying out louder for someone to help me, but no one answers.

I run my crusty palm through my hair and realize it is shorter. I stop in the middle of darkness and sit on the pavement on the middle of the cracks of the sidewalk. My hair is tangled and short and full of leaves from the ground. I break into a painful cry when another man walks by me. He keeps on walking by, faster, almost running.

"Can you help me—please?!"

He ignores my cries and runs. He runs from my coldness, from my desperation.

I look up and notice there is a large avenue in front of me. I walk some more. I find a bus bench and sit. There is a supermarket next to me and a vacant parking lot and lots of street lights. I see a police car, and I wave as he drives on by. He waves back, never stopping to my cries or pleas for help. I want to be saved. I want to find my home, my warm bed where I can lie and wake from this nightmare.

Across the boulevard I see a gas station, and I pick myself up, nearly blinded by a vicious wave of pain. There is no wind at this moment, but I feel like it's twenty below zero. The road is four lanes, but it might as well be four miles. I don't remember if I looked both ways before making my way to the other side, yet somehow, I do, dragging one foot then another.

Another police car parks and the policeman enters the convenience store. The attendant sees me through the glass, comes out, and starts yelling.

"Don't even think of entering my store! Don't even think of coming close to the door!"

I beg him to call the cop so that I can explain to him that I am lost, but he just keeps yelling that no way is a drug addict going to enter his store, especially on his shift. He tells me to go away. He motions to the road. He claps and shakes his hands outward. I don't move.

Finally, he goes inside and calls the officer. I see him pointing to me like a witness pointing to a criminal. I sit on the curb with my head in between my knees. I can't breathe. What drug addict was he talking about? Then again, maybe I am a drug addict. Maybe that's why I can't remember where I am.

The cop takes one look at me and begins to ask for my information. He calls for back-up and is agitated that he has to take care of me since he has just come off his shift. As he calls this into the station, he makes it very clear that he is on his way home. He has the right to go home, and I am merely an inconvenience. Without getting up I explain to him that I am lost, all the while pulling at my hair to ease the strain of pain shooting in it.

He yells at me to get up. It's a struggle, but I do what he says. If I do, maybe he will take me home.

He asks for my name, address, and telephone number, then, with a look downward, he asks what's in the front pocket of my shorts. I hadn't noticed anything, but now I push down on the pockets. He grabs his pistol on the side of his hip.

"Ma'am, get your hands up. Do you have any drugs on you? Do you have any needles in your pockets? Do you have any weapons?"

I stare at him, hands raised, shaking with uncertainty because I have no idea what's in my pockets. He watches me warily as I bring a hand down to feel what is there, only to give up, exhausted. He takes over the search, pulls a small wallet from my front pocket, and asks me if it is mine. I don't recognize it; I say as I sit back down on the curb. He yells to get back up, but I can't. I'm too faint and cold and scared and weak. I cry, trying to explain between sobs that I am disoriented and that I want my husband to come get me. I give the cop our house number, my husband's work number, and even his social security number. I give the officer all the answers he needs to get me home. All I want is to climb into my bed and forget this nightmare.

More troopers arrive. I hear the sound of an ambulance in the distance. I can't move. I am treated like a criminal, and no one seems to want to listen to what I have to say. Am I a criminal? Am I an addict? What has happened to me? Am I a drunk who can't remember how I ended up in a park? I am here, but I am not.

The officers speak among themselves, referring to me as if I am not there. They believe I am a homeless woman, a prostitute, or a drug addict. They believe my memory loss is due to drinking or drugging. They believe I am crazy. There are people around me now, but I am just as alone as when I walked that empty sidewalk.

The cop shows me a license with a strange address on it. He shoves it in my face, along with his flashlight.

"Is this your address?"

Unable to look up, I answer no, then give him the address to my apartment again. He asks if I walked from that address all the way to this gas station. Before I can reply he informs me that it is well over twenty miles. I know I'd walked a lot, but that distance sounds extreme. Another cop asks if I had anything else in my pants. I struggle to get up and check, then shake my head.

"No."

As they go through the wallet, they find a picture of a woman with six children posing around her. They find some money. They find credit cards, my social security card. More pictures of kids. No pictures of me or my husband. He shoves the picture of the woman with kids under my face.

"Is this you, Mildred? Are these your children?"

I look at the picture.

"I have no children, and that woman is not me."

My vision is blurry, and if I don't lie down, I will pass out. I am cold, and I am tired. I am here, but I am not.

The interrogations continue while the paramedic puts a flashlight into my eyes.

"What year is it?"

"It's 1987, and I have a headache and need to lie down. I can't breathe. I am cold." I am shaking and ready to throw up.

"Mildred, you can't lie down. Where did you walk from? Have you been sexually assaulted tonight? Where did you get the bump on your forehead and the cuts on your elbows and knees? Did you get into a fight with someone? Did your spouse hurt you?"

I can't breathe. I place my head in between my legs again, and the ache from my forehead, my knees, and the back of my head seems to embody me in a blanket of fury. I want to vomit. I want the foul smell of dirt to go away. The blood has dried up on my skin. My hands feel like sandpaper as I rub my face. My nails are full of dirt, bitten to the core, and blackness is inside the edges. My elbows are rough with sand and dirt. My toes are dirty as they sit inside the flip flops. I never wear open-toed shoes. I've hated my toes since I was a child, and this saddens me more with a realization that I am not me. My legs have thick stubbles poking through. I am not the woman I was yesterday. I am someone else. I am here. I am not here tonight.

"Mildred…"

I interrupt him. I know he's on a roll.

"Please help me. Call my husband's work at Domino's Pizza and tell him to come get me. Tell him that I woke up in a park and can't find the way back home. Please call him and tell him to bring me a jacket."

"Mildred, how did you get all those cuts? Did you fall and hit your head? Did you do drugs tonight?"

The paramedic begins to run a line to give me oxygen, but first I have to take a breathalyzer test and walk a straight line to make sure I am not under the influence of alcohol. Am I an addict?

I barely pass the test. I can't stand up and walk a straight line. I have no alcohol in my system. The test shows this. I tell them what I know. I tell them that I am here, but that my memory is not. I cannot make sense of anything. As I tell my story, I know they must think I sound like a lunatic...because it's how I sound to myself.

I woke up in a park. I thought it was the park near my apartment, but I couldn't find my street. I couldn't find my building. I tell them I was alone when I woke up at the park. I don't know anything else. I don't know what time I got there. I don't know anything. I don't know why or how I ended up on the pavement. I don't know how long I was there or if someone left me there. I don't know anything. I just want to go home. I don't know this city, where everything looks so new. I can't understand anything they want me to hear.

The first officer is now less aggressive and more curious as to what might have happened to me.

"Do you know what park you woke up in? Do you know the street? Did anyone hurt you? Did you see anyone around you? Was the park closed when you left? Can you remember if you were completely dressed when you woke up?"

"I woke up just like you see me now. I don't know the rest. I don't know anything. I am scared. I am dizzy. I want to lie down."

I hear more questions. I hear them talking but can't understand them. I can't understand their attitude towards me. I can't understand why they don't hear what I am saying. They are listening to my sounds, but they are not hearing.

I begin to cry harder and tell them I don't know anything more than what I have told them. I don't see anything else. I don't think. I am dead, but I am still breathing.

"Mrs. Mestril, how old are you?"

"I am nineteen."

"Ma'am, when is your birthday?"

"April 17, 1968." I pull on my hair as if releasing the pain from the inside.

He looks down at me with a bewildered stare, then a smirk forms on his lips. "Ma'am, you are not nineteen."

He shows me the license again, and the picture is not me. It is some other version of me. It is an older woman with similar features. It is not me. I am not her.

"Who is this woman on your license?"

"I don't know. I don't recognize that address either. I live on Lincoln Street in Hollywood, Florida. I don't know where this city on the license is. Can't you just call the numbers I gave you and let me go home? You can go home too." I give them my mother's telephone number. She's my last resort. I struggle with this because I know she will be pissed.

I think for a moment at the stupidity of their questions. I am tired. I am cold, and the more I hold my head up the more I slip away. I will wake up. I will laugh at this dream. I will laugh when I wake up and tell Nathan about a stupid dream of my being older and lost. We will laugh at the stupidity. He will tell me what he always tells me:

"You have some fucked up dreams, you know that? Your mind is fucking psychotic when you sleep. Thankfully, it's not like that when you are awake. It was only a dream."

I will laugh at the comment, then I will get up for work and leave him to sleep through the morning. I will be me again.

The questions continue, and I am brought back to this moment.

"What year did you say we are in?"

Chapter 1

"It's 1987. I need to lie down, sir."

"What month are we in?"

"It's October."

"Mildred, it's November of 2001. And from the birth date on your license, you are thirty-three years old."

He says something I can't hear to the other officer. I hear their radio, the dispatcher. I hear everything. I hear the noises of cars passing by on the boulevard. I hear the sounds of air passing through my ears. Then I hear nothing. I blank out his words. It can't be that many years later than I think it is. I lie on the cement, unable to keep my head up any longer. I am shivering. My ass is cold; my back is even colder. The officer who was annoyed with the evening's interruption suggests to the paramedics that they take me to the hospital. The two telephone numbers I had given them are incorrect. The pizzeria has no one there with my husband's name. No one knows who I am. They don't know what to do with me. They can't take me to a shelter because I have cuts and blood and bumps that make no sense to them. They call in a Mildred Mestril, but the only address is that of Southwest Ranches. They will send an officer to that house. They will find someone else is the owner of the wallet, of the license, of the pictures, and of that life.

I find darkness. I find myself half-conscious riding in an ambulance. I can hear the voices of the paramedics assuming the worst of me. I am probably a prostitute and got beat up and left in a park. Or I took a drug and fell asleep on a park bench. All the assumptions add to the uncertainty that I am not me, and this is a nightmare. I am alive but dead. I am with people but alone. I am disoriented and scared. I am asleep, but I am awake. With the oxygen mask on my face, I doze off again. I am here but I am not.

CHAPTER 2

I open my eyes to the lights of an emergency room. The lights hurt my eyes. I feel raw and naked and overexposed. Panic and anxiety rush in again, forcing the heart to push up against my throat. I pull the oxygen mask off and call out for a nurse. I see one passing by. I have an ID band on my wrist, Band-Aids on my elbows, and an IV running from my arm. I am in a hospital gown. I can see the redness in my arm where they drew blood. I can hear the chaos of the emergency room. I am here, but I am not. I can't remember what they've done to me.

A nurse checks in on me. I ask in a low voice.

"Miss, where am I?"

She adjusts the monitors and makes sure my IV is okay.

"Miss, where am I? I need to see my husband."

I try to pull myself up, but the pain in my head pulls me back down. I notice the nurse's uniform but I can't focus my vision to read the letters on the tag hanging from her neck.

"Mildred, you are in Memorial Hospital."

She touches my wrist gently. She checks my pulse. I am no longer cold. I am no longer alone. I am still scared.

"I need to have you sign the admission forms. We got your insurance information from your wallet. Do you remember what happened to you?"

"I don't know. I woke up in a park. I want my husband. Please, please call my husband. He must be so worried. I can give you all his information. He has a beeper. Can you try his beeper?"

"That's your husband sitting right there."

She points to an older gentleman who has a tired, worried expression. He sits across from the bed staring at me. I hadn't noticed him sitting there. He could be my father but I know my father and he is not him. I ignore her comment. I ignore the old man.

"No, you are mistaken—that's not my husband. My husband is a young man, just like me. He is tall and thin and has curly black hair and a mustache. His name is Nathan Mestril."

I continue to give her his work telephone number, his beeper number, the house information. She quickly interrupts me.

"Mildred, what year do you think this is?"

"What is it with everyone and the year? It is 1987, and I need to see the doctor. I need to talk to the doctor. I want to know why I have a bump in the back of my head. I want some Tylenol or something stronger to take away the nausea and pain shooting from my head."

I am angry. I had been treated like a criminal, like I am crazy, and finally been told that it is a different year, and I am married to a man who could be my father.

The older man never speaks. He just sits there, concerned and maybe angry, dangling his crossed leg. He has on black jeans and a blue t-shirt. He does not move from his position on the chair. I stare at him, waiting for a comment or input different from what the nurse has said. Nothing comes out of him. I see his hair is mostly white and thinning. He looks down at the floor, still moving his leg back and forth. I look at him and say nothing. He is here but he is not.

I stare at the people walking outside of my space through the green curtains. They are dressed so differently from what I know. Fashion has changed from yesterday. What is going on? I read the ID bracelet on my wrist. I read, but I don't comprehend the date, the year. I tug on it and let it go. I tug on it and let it go down with my arm against my body. I am living in an episode of *The Twilight Zone*. I cannot grasp this reality. It is not real.

I yell for the nurse again. I need more answers, different answers. She comes back impatiently.

"Ma'am, there is nothing I can tell you. You just relax and wait for the doctor to come see you. He has been called in. It is early morning, and he is due in around nine."

She rushes out, leaving me alone with the silent stranger again. He stares at the floor. He stares past me. He is here, but he is not.

I fall asleep again. When I awake, I am being wheeled on the stretcher into a room to get a CAT scan of my head. I assume someone is going to explain the bump on the back of my head and the scratches everywhere. My body feels bruised and mangled, even though I don't seem to have anything broken. I can move my legs and arms. I just can't remember anything before waking up in the park. The hospital will fix me. I will go home. The hospital will realize that I am not crazy when they get in touch with Nate.

Somewhere between all the medical tests my impatient mind wanders off. I am back in the ER.

An old woman enters the emergency room, and as she approaches my bed, I realize with a start that she is my mother. She has aged so much overnight!

"Mami, what's happened to you?" I ask abruptly as she leans in to kiss my forehead, "Why are you so old?"

I wince then, because the kiss has sent pain tearing down my spine.

"Oh, Millie, what happened to you? You left last night, and I was asleep, and then Jorge woke me up this morning to tell me that you were in the hospital. What happened? Why did you go on a walk so late at night? Why didn't you wake me up and tell me you were going out?"

"What walk? Who's Jorge? And what do you mean, *Why I didn't wake you?* I don't understand…"

I begin to cry. She sits on the bed and holds me. I don't want to be held. I want to go home to my husband. I want to crawl into my bed and fall asleep.

She doesn't grasp the reality—my lack of memory. She doesn't understand. I don't either. She speaks, ignoring my cries. The tears hurt coming out. My eyes feel swollen. I hate that she's upset. I see her so small and fragile. I see her, but I don't.

"I am living with you and the kids and Jorge. You don't remember? I moved in last month because we are moving into the big ranch. Remember the ranch? Remember the beautiful house Jorge is building? Remember your horses and your garden?"

I am confused, and I try to make out what she's talking about. I try briefly to analyze her words, her tone, her look, and her lies. I can't.

"Mom, where is Nathan? Why does the nurse say that that man sitting over there is my husband? Who is that man, Jorge, you are talking about?"

I squeeze her hands, noting again how much she has aged. Her once lovely hands are bent and full of knobs. Her hair is completely white, and she is much smaller—a vanishing version of the mother I had yesterday. I lean back on the bed. I am exhausted. I do not want to hear anything, and I beg her to take me to my apartment. I beg her to call Nate.

Agitated and losing patience, she answers bluntly, not watching her words but pouring them out without noticing the hurt they will bring. They are sharp swords with syllables that break through my skin.

"Nathan is no longer in your life. It has been many years. You are thirty-three years old and have six children. You are not a teenager anymore. You have to put yourself together and get better

16

quickly because those kids need you today when they get home. I will not be telling them that you are in the hospital and have lost your memory. You have a business to run. You have to close on the sale of the house you live in now so you can move to the ranch in two weeks. You can't do this to us. You can't do this to them. You've got to get up and get going. You have to stop this nonsense because there is no time for a breakdown. That is a luxury you do not have right now."

I tune her out. Nothing has changed. This is who she is. This is who I am. Nothing has changed since yesterday. But everything has.

I do not take the news about my age seriously, and the stupidity of having children seems more amusing than disturbing. I am nineteen, and in no way do I have six children. I am trying to get pregnant. Nate and I have been trying for months. I have gotten pregnant in the past, but lost the baby in the first trimester. I run my hand over my stomach. It doesn't feel like mine. These thoughts go through me on and on as her words slip out.

I shock myself by voicing my thoughts to her. I never do this. I am here, but I am not. I have courage to speak to her like never before. The guilt is far away. I can't believe how removed from it I am.

"Mami, I am nineteen. I just got married last year. We don't have any kids. Mom, please stop pretending. This is no joke."

She comes to hold me, but I don't want her to. I can't forget the hell she put me through the year before. I can't forget our differences. I can't forget her bigotry toward Nathan, who was biracial. How she demanded I break it off with the Black Cuban man while presenting herself to the world as accepting of other races, and the fights we had because I was so enraged by her hypocrisy. I can't forget that I left and have barely spoken to her since then. I knew she'd lost weight, that she had been sick, but I couldn't believe how much she had aged in such a short time. I feel the guilt come through me... and the anger. *I know she just doesn't want to call my husband.*

17

She wants to control this. She wants to control me. She's meddling again while taking advantage of this situation.

"Mami, who's taking care of Abuelo and Abuela?"

She tells me my grandparents died a few years ago and I shake my head in disbelief. I sob. I insist on seeing a doctor. Any doctor will do. I push my mother gently off the bed and turn to stare at the beige wall while tears fall rapidly. I am frustrated and annoyed. I am a victim of someone's oversight. Someone has made a mistake, and I am paying for it, here in this sterile room, in a different world.

"I don't want to talk to you right now. You don't make any sense. Everyone here is trying to make me go crazy. I am not crazy or stupid, and all I've gotten tonight is a bunch of bullshit. I am tired. I am fucking tired of this nonsense. I am sick. I need to throw up."

The smell of the hospital overtakes me. I can feel the juices in my stomach gather and rush up and down.

My mother tells me to lower my voice, demands that I not curse. She gives me a bedpan to throw up and I gag, but nothing comes out. The sickness runs through my body like little pins poking through every cell. I lie back on the bed. I watch her. I watch what's become of her. I search for familiarity and can't find anything right now.

She goes to talk to the man across the room. He still hasn't said anything. He looks like a guard, waiting for me to move so he could restrain me. They mumble, and though I can't hear what they are saying I know they are conspiring. I am too tired to yell. The coldness falls on me again, the lights above blind me. I breathe deeply and watch them exchange the wallet found in my pocket. I watch how they go through it and discuss if there is anything missing. They are dissecting it. They look over at me, and they are dissecting me too.

He starts to explain to my now-elderly mother in Spanish his version of my story. I can understand him clearly. I close my eyes and concentrate on his words. I am surprised at how much I can understand. I always hated when my mother spoke to me in Spanish.

I would always answer in English. No one could imagine I was Puerto Rican. My Spanish is broken, and I intertwine it with my English, pissing off those who can't understand English even more. I am a disgrace for being Hispanic and not speaking it. Tonight, I am a disgrace for being in this bed, for inconveniencing them. I am a disgrace to myself for allowing this moment and not getting to the bottom of the truth.

"Carmen, I don't understand what happened to her," the man was saying. "I went to shower, and she was gone. I noticed she didn't take her purse or her keys. The car was still outside. When she did not come back after an hour, I went looking for her in the neighborhood. I then got in my car and went to the ranch to see if she had walked there. Then as I was pulling out a police car was pulling in. They asked me if I knew her and showed me her license. They told me she was picked up in Pines Boulevard and brought here. That was well after midnight, and so I came over. She was found crossing the street into a gas station in front of Walmart. They told me she's lost her memory."

My mother asks him a few more questions. She tells him she is very concerned about the kids. She doesn't understand what he has said. She doesn't seem to believe him. She begins to drill him. Nothing has changed. Her questions are still asked in the same manner. She asks but doesn't pay attention to the answer. She just keeps asking the same thing with different words in order to get the answer she expects.

"Jorge, did you have a fight? How come she went walking so late?"

"We had an argument, but then I went to take a shower and she was watching television."

"What was the argument about? How late did you come home? I didn't hear you come in."

I can't hear anything after that. My mind goes blank.

I am not me. I am not married to that man. I do not have any children. I am a teenager. I am a married woman. I work at a bank. I am me, but I am not.

I sleep for some time. When I wake, I call for the nurse again. I see I am alone. My mother and the man are gone. The nurse checks the monitors. I grab her arm softly.

"Yes, what do you need, Mildred?"

"I need you to call the following telephone and ask for Nathan."

I try to whisper a number but she interrupts—not unkindly, but sternly.

"If you can answer the following question and get it right, I will call for you, who's the President of the United States?"

I think she is joking.

"What?"

"Who's the President?"

"Ronald Regan."

"Nope, it's George Bush."

"George Bush is Vice President."

She laughs, winks at me, and walks out. She never takes down the phone number.

My mother walks in with the man a little while later. They sit down and hold their own conversation. A few minutes later a doctor walks in, x-rays in hand. He heads straight for my mother and the man, telling them, in a beautiful Caribbean accent, that he is my neurologist. Then he comes over to me and introduces himself with many formalities that I really have no use for.

"My name is Doctor Suite."

"Sweet like candy?" I ask, not to be snarky, but because I really am curious about the spelling.

"No, like a hotel suite, but it is pronounced the same. How are you feeling, Mildred? Can you remember what happened to you?"

I shake my head.

"No."

"How did you get the bumps on your head? Did someone hurt you? Can you tell me the last thing or the first thing you remember tonight?"

"Doctor, I woke up in a park. My head hurt. My hands were scraped, and my knees were bleeding. I was face-down on the pavement. I don't know how I ended up there. I walked for a long time. I asked for help, and no one helped me. I then saw a cop and crossed a big street to ask for help. I was treated horribly. No one seemed to want to help me…" I start to cry uncontrollably.

He touches my hand, gestures for me to calm down. He says that I am in a safe place. Everything is going to be alright.

"Nothing is alright. I can't remember anything. My husband apparently is nowhere to be found. I don't want to be here. I want to go home."

"What is the last memory you have right now? Tell me what you remember that you think happened recently."

"I went on vacation about two weeks ago with my husband to visit my mother's cousin in Ocala. It was my husband's twentieth birthday."

He points towards the man by my mother.

"Do you remember that gentleman next to your mother?"

I shake my head. "No. No. No!"

"Now, you listen to me, okay?"

"I don't know what happened to you exactly, but you have some amnesia."

I interrupt. "As opposed to a lot of amnesia?"

He laughs.

I did not mean it to be funny. I want to know the difference, but I let him have his moment. I say nothing.

"We are going to run some more tests today, and hopefully after you rest a little, you'll get your memory back, okay?"

He smiles and speaks with the only certainty I have heard all evening.

"What time is it, doctor?"

"It's almost 10:30 a.m.," he replies, adding, "It is November 8, 2001."

"Can you give me something for my headache?"

"Sure, I will tell the nurse to put it in your IV. You just rest, Mildred, and I'll be back later today to check on you. We are going to get you into a room, and hopefully with a lot of rest you'll get your memory back soon. Now take it easy."

He says goodbye me, then asks my mother and the man to come outside.

The nurse comes in and injects liquid into the IV. Within minutes I am gone.

CHAPTER 3

When I wake up there is a tray of food in front of me on the table; my mother is sitting next to the man. I stare at them, drugged up but feeling calm.

I tell my mother I want to go home; she says that I have to get better first. When she sees me struggle, unsuccessfully, to sit up, she starts crying again. I feel sorry for having to put her through whatever it is that I am going through, but no matter how hard I try to recall the evening I cannot make sense of it.

A nurse comes in and checks my monitor, then takes my blood pressure. I have been poked, pulled, and examined from head to toe. I ask her to bring the TV closer so that I can watch it, but I can't find anything remotely familiar on any station.

I see the man walking toward me and realize my mother has left us alone. He brings the chair and sits so I can hear him. He speaks to me for the first time. It is in Spanish.

"Are you feeling better?"

I stare at him. There is nothing familiar in his eyes. I can't find a trace of me in them.

"Who exactly are you to me?" I ask as I turn off the television and move it out of the way.

"I am your boyfriend. We've been together for almost eleven years. We are not legally married but we live together and have a business together. It's easier to say we are married."

He hesitates a moment and then starts up again, his brown eyes glossy with tears.

"Do you really not remember me?"

"Are we really living together?"

"Yes." This yes is full of pain.

"I don't remember you, sir."

"How can you not remember me? We have a life together. We have six children. You don't remember your children?"

Six children! I am too young to have that many kids. My eyes watering, I lie back on the pillow and look away from him. I am silent. Why would I want all those kids? I wanted to have ten kids when I was a child but never imagined actually having them as a young adult.

I answer with tears rolling down my face.

"No, I don't remember your kids."

"They aren't mine. They are yours. You had two boys in your marriage with your husband and then adopted four orphans from Romania. They are your life. You are a wonderful mother. How can you not recall the kids?"

That question tugs inside my heart, but the truth is, I am being told a story about a woman who has a much older boyfriend/husband and six kids. It isn't a fact about my life, just a story about someone who they think I am. I am here, but I am not. I am alone in my thoughts. It's as if fate is playing a cruel joke of hide-and-seek with me, and I am losing.

"Look, Jorge—is that your name? I can't remember you, or the kids, or any job."

I pause, trying to compose myself. I feel as if I am drifting away slowly from this moment. I feel as though I am losing my mind.

"I am tired of people saying I remember and just don't want to admit it. I have been treated as if I am mentally ill. This is not a joke from me to you or my mother. I don't understand why my mother looks so old. I don't understand how I woke up in some park late at night. I can't, for the life of me, comprehend how I have lost fourteen years of my life. I am sad to think my marriage is over and that he is no longer in my life, especially right now when I need him." I lie back on the pillow, staring ahead. "I want to know why."

Jorge brings his seat closer to my bed.

"Millie, I'm the one who doesn't understand. Why did you storm out of our house?"

"You tell me, Jorge. I want to know what you did to me that would make me leave. Or what did I do that I had to leave? Do I normally take walks late at night? I don't know you. I see you, and I can't find a single memory of you. I can't."

The tears are coming harder now. They come with fear. They come down with anxiety. His demeanor has a flashing light that silently warns me to stop talking.

He does not answer, and in that silence, I understand that my life isn't that different after all. The dance is still the same. My partner, though he has a different face and a different name, is the same as well, and I am in the same submissive role. This awareness arrives quickly in spite of my confusion.

We talk on and off until late in the afternoon. He tries to tell me about the business. He tries to make me aware of my life now. I hear him but can't comprehend what he is saying to me. I speak to him in English and he gets me to change to Spanish. I am shocked to find myself speaking it fluently. This is not me. I am not the one talking like this. I can't speak without noticing the phrases that now, so easily, move through my tongue. I am alone in thoughts that pertain to me, without me.

Finally, he stands and says he has to go. He has business to tend to, plus he needs to be at the house when the kids get home from school. I am relieved. I am tired and need to sleep. The medication is wearing off, and my head is throbbing. I need to be alone. I am alone.

CHAPTER 4

By evening the emergency room has died down some. Doctor Suite comes in and tells me that I have company. Jorge and my mother have brought the children to visit me. I still have not been moved to a normal room. The doctor explains to me that the children expect to see their mother. A mother who remembers they exist; a mother who knows each one by name, by face, and by memory.

"Mildred, this is a traumatic experience for everyone. Just relax and see if you can remember them, okay? Be nice, and if you can't recall any of them, try and pretend. Don't force yourself to remember, but just let the moment sink in."

I nod and smile and say, "Okay."

Five children enter the room with shocked looks on their faces. I don't bother to ask where the sixth child is since I am too busy trying to be nice. Some of them start to cry. Some just stand in horror. One just stares at my blank expression. My head hurts. I stare in shock too. My body feels weak, and I am tired of trying to remember anything from the past fourteen years. Whenever I try to go past nineteen there is a wall in front. I cannot climb over it. I have to focus on more energy than I am prepared to give. It seems everything has been erased, that the people standing around me are actors in some play, and I am doing the best acting job possible. These are not my children. They are someone else's problems. I am hoping that they will find their real mother and that I can go back to the life I remember. I am hoping that this is some weird dream and that when I wake, I have nothing to do but laugh at this situation. I am in a room full of people, but I am alone.

One by one they come to kiss me. I let them. The youngest one hugs me and starts crying. The lady who takes care of them comes over and kisses me and begins a conversation in Spanish with so much pity that it is overwhelming. I want no pity. I want answers to my many questions. I want them gone. I feel for them. I feel for me. In a room full of people, I am lacking the air to breathe.

After meeting them I have the satisfaction that they aren't mine. None of them look like me. None of them look like my husband. Their very existence is irrelevant to my life. I manage to spend the longest ten minutes in their presence until I lie back and tell the doctor that I am tired. They depart with many goodbyes.

"Get better soon, Mommy!"

"Can't wait to have you home!"

"Can we come back tomorrow? Can we stay with you, Mom?"

My thoughts create a mountain of panic and fear that paralyzes me for the rest of the night. I am not their mother. I am not me. I am not a thirty-three-year-old woman who manages their lives.

The doctor comes in and tells me that because they can't figure out how I lost my memory he needs to rule out every medical explanation.

"I am going to do a spinal tap on you."

"What's that?"

"I am going to draw spinal fluid from your spine. I need to make sure you don't have meningitis. Meningitis can cause brain damage and amnesia. There will be a little discomfort, but I will be quick. I need for you to lie on your stomach."

I turn over. He opens my robe. He places some liquid and numbs the area. It is cold.

"You are just going to feel a little pinch."

"Okay."

"Are you ready? Don't move, okay."

A nurse stands next to me. I dig my hands into the pillow.

"Okay."

I feel the needle break through my skin. It reaches the bottom of my spine. I feel him pulling back on the syringe. It is pulling back on my nerves. I breathe in and out heavily. He is taking my soul with him. I feel dizzy. I feel cold. I feel an emptiness slipping out and a heaviness slipping in.

I begin to have flashes of memories of being a sick child in hospitals in Puerto Rico. I can smell the medicines, the sheets, the blood. And, then I am back to the present moment.

"Almost done, but I need to take from another location as well."

"Okay. Please be quick. I feel sick."

"You are doing good, Mildred. Is it Mildred or Millie?"

"Millie. Are you making small talk now, Doc?"

"Yes."

I dig deeper into the bed with wet hands from cold sweats. I turn my head to the other side. I tell myself not to be afraid. I tell myself to take it like a woman. I have always hated needles in spite of the many that my body has endured. I need to take it in and then let it out.

He numbs another area. I feel the pain go up my spine and down to my ass. I feel a tingle in my legs and a burning in my arms. I want it to stop. I want to throw up on the pillow. I am sweating all over. I am slipping into water, dissolving into the bed. I feel lightheaded. My blood pressure is…

"Are you almost done, Doc?"

"Almost."

He removes everything and tells me to lie back on the bed, flat. I am not to move for several hours.

"Now, Mildred, if you move the little holes can't repair themselves. You will have a small headache in a little while. I am going to give you something in the IV so you can sleep."

"What happens if I move?"

"Well, try not to. The fluid can leak through your spine and cause you tremendous discomfort. You may have a bad headache. Just lie there still for a while."

"Okay. I'm glad I went to the bathroom already."

He laughs.

"I will see you tomorrow. They have a room for you. Feel better and rest."

He taps my shoulder and says goodbye.

"Goodnight, Doctor."

He leaves.

I am alone.

I am trying to get my life back. I need to get my lifeline back into my spine, into my head, into my heart.

CHAPTER 5

Sometime in the middle of the night, I wake up—thankfully in a private room—and make my way to the bathroom, gliding the IV holder beside me. I close the door and sit on the toilet. I am sick to my stomach, and I am beginning to feel that slight headache Dr. Suite told me about. After peeing what seems a gallon, I get up, flush the toilet, and drag the apparatus to the sink. The lights are bright. I wash my hands and slowly look up to the mirror, feeling a rush of panic to see a stranger staring back at me.

I touch my face. The reflection does the same. I begin to cry. Where did my youth go off to? Dazed, I keep touching my cheeks, my forehead. I see the bump. I have a scratch over my right brow. I have more freckles and worry lines, and I am overweight. I touch my body. I feel its heaviness. I open the gown and stare down at my breasts. They have scars. I look at them in the mirror, standing on tippy toes trying to reach the reflection. The scars look like arks dragging from my nipples to the bottom of my breasts. I stare long and hard, trying to find the woman I know is nineteen. She's gone. I sit on the toilet and sob. I grab my chest as if my heart is falling out. I am dreaming. This is another messed-up dream. I run my hand again over my hair, pulling it back hard to release the pain. It does nothing but create more questions about the length, the color, and the texture.

Where did I go? What happened to my life? How did I become this woman? My head aches. I get up to the mirror again. My eyes are swollen from so much crying. I can't understand how years could be completely erased. I see more freckles on my nose, and my hair is so short, and the ends are dry. My skin is dry. I touch it. I pinch it. I poke it. My nose and mouth and chin seem fuller. I stare down at my thighs. They are bigger and my stomach is not flat. I am not nineteen.

I begin to talk to God. I am so loud that a nurse comes to knock on the door. I don't care. I demand answers from Him, wanting to know when I will wake up. Then I'm begging Him to wake me up from this nightmare. I am scared. I do not want to be living with another man, an older man, and six children. I do not want what's ahead of me in this parallel dimension. I want me to be me the way I remember me. I want to experience my own childbirth. I want more intimacy with Nate. I want to make things right between us. I want to travel. I want to remember. I want me.

The nurse comes into the bathroom and helps me back to my bed. The whole time, I am sobbing and begging her to find my husband, *not* the man who had been there earlier that evening. I go through the telephone numbers again, the address, the details of my husband's employment. If there is any hope of recovery, I have to find out the truth, why my life is so different from the one I had wanted when I was younger. I had wanted to be an artist, I tell her, I had already been accepted to the Art Institute in Paris and was going to study there. I wanted to see Ireland. I had gotten married a year earlier and decided to study medicine. I'd had dreams of giving birth to our first child before I was twenty. I was told I may not be able to have children and needed to try as young as possible.

She doesn't write anything down. She is hearing me, but not listening. She leaves me on my bed, checks the monitors, and exits into a world I cannot relate to. I begin to feel an inexplicable sorrow that pushes my heart to beat against my rib cage. I can feel panic taking over. I don't know how to stop it. I am overcome with fear. I can hear the machine beeping beside me as my blood pressure begins to rise. I can hear the noise beneath the silence of the sterile room. I can hear the buzzing of electronics. I can't hear my memories. I am alone.

A little while later, while the panic is at its highest, another nurse comes in to check on me. She touches my hand and asks if I need anything. She pulls the chair across the room closer to my bed. She sits comfortably. She has time. She's on break. Her name is Cinthya, and I notice the awkward spelling on her tag.

I tell her my story, and she lets me. I tell her what I know. I also tell her what I have been told and don't believe is true.

"What do you think happened to you last night?" she asks.

"I don't really know."

"And you don't want to know, do you?"

"No. I want my life back. The only life I have in my memory."

"And you will. Give it time."

Cinthya is a bodacious black woman probably in her forties. She is beautiful, and speaks with the lilting tone of the Caribbean. She is kind. She is there. I am not alone.

"Imagine waking up fourteen years from today. How would you feel?"

"I hope I've hit the damn lotto." She smiles and lights the room in a way that makes me think that I have been given some strong painkillers.

I smile through the tears. I smile wiping them away. My face is soaked. The tears feel like blood pouring out from me.

"Seriously, how would *you* feel?" I ask while she sits with her hands on her thighs.

"I can't say. I guess I would be scared. I would feel isolated. But give it time, girl. Give it time. Your memory will come back. You are still so young. It's not like if you woke up thirty years later. It's not so bad, if you ask me. I wouldn't mind forgetting some years from my life. Heck, consider it a giant blessing. Enjoy it while you can. Everything happens for a reason. Nothing goes unnoticed in your life. These are the events that mold you, make you, and force you to evolve to a higher spiritual level. Maybe you've been praying for a break in this life, and here it is. You don't know until you know."

I don't find it possible to see it as a blessing, but I'm still smiling. Her words come out in humor and they comfort me. There is magic in her face. There is certainty in her words.

She gets up and comes to touch my hands. Then, holding them between her own, she says a little prayer I can't make out. She quickly lets them fall against my stomach and touches my head. I feel the heat in her hands and the pain subsides into a mild discomfort.

"If you need anything press that button, but try and rest. Answers and clarity come through silence. Try to quiet the mind. You have forgotten this life, so take advantage of the vacation."

I have nothing to say to these words.

"Thank you," I mumble, already beginning to drift off, "Thank you for listening."

"You are welcome, my beloved child."

She leaves. I leave. I am at peace.

CHAPTER 6

I dream. In darkness, I see pieces of a giant jigsaw puzzle. I work diligently trying to fit the many pieces together and I am frustrated because some seem to be missing. I cry and scream, then everything goes black. Suddenly I am being grabbed by a man. He begins beating me, then pushes me in a ditch. He rips my clothes off. He sticks his hand in my vagina and rips it apart. I yell. I scream. He is killing me. No one comes to my help. No one hears me. I am alone.

I wake up to light sneaking through the green blinds. I am safe. My heart is racing. I try to grab on to what is real, only in this moment I can't decipher what that is. I rub my forehead. I touch the bump. I touch my head. I feel the bump under my head. This is real. I touch my thighs. I am alive. This is real. This is where I am. I am not me. I am back to being someone else.

I try to gather strength to enter this new day. I know I can't go back to who I am without accepting who I've become, but the woman staring back at me in the mirror is still a stranger. The dream has drained me. I am torn between what's here and what's not. I am torn between the violence and this reality. I close my eyes and wish for the bed to suck me in. I can't analyze the night's vision. I don't want to. I can't analyze the day's nightmare. I don't want to.

For some reason I can't hold my head up straight. The pain is unbearable. It travels down my spine. It hurts when I sit, when I get up, when I lie back down. I can't find comfort. I can't find me.

I get up to go to the bathroom. I vomit. Over and over, I let the liquid flow out. Somewhere inside is the real me. Somewhere now, not back in time. Back in bed, I lie perfectly still, afraid if I move, I won't find the small comfort I have right now. The phone rings. I answer and lie back.

"Hello."

"How are you feeling, sweetheart?"

My mother is calling early. My mother knows no time. She has zero boundaries.

"Somewhat."

"Did you sleep good?"

"No."

She hears me. She is not listening.

"I will be there after I get the kids off to school. Do you want anything from home? Do you want any food? You want your pajamas? Do you need anything?"

"My memory."

She laughs.

"Aside from that, Millie. Glad you are feeling better."

"No, Mom. Nothing."

She doesn't notice the sarcasm. She doesn't notice I am not there. How can a mother not notice the difference?

"Are you okay?"

"No. I am in pain. I can't talk. I feel sick."

I hang up then, not wanting to hear anymore. I lie back and tears roll down my face, not knowing which hurts more, my body or my mind. I lie there, sifting through random memories of my past. It is a past from long ago, but to me it feels like yesterday.

The door opens, and a nurse's aide brings in food, along with a paper for me to pick out my other meals for the day. I tell her I can't eat. She says I need to fill in the paper. I don't. I leave the food on the table. I can't eat. I can't sit. I am sick.

The phone rings again. I let it. I don't want to talk.

It rings and rings. It stops. It rings and rings. It stops. The ring goes through me like nails. The noise, the light, and the nausea bring me to hyperventilating. I push the button for the nurse. I push and push until she answers. I can't speak. I reach for a bedpan and throw up. It's clear fluid. It's water. Nothing has been in my stomach. It might as well be blood. It is taking my life with each release.

A different nurse enters and tries to clean me up. I don't want to be cleaned up. I want something for the pain. I am shivering. I am cold. I am alone again with my thoughts. I am alone again in hell. I ask her to please tell Cinthya to come see me before she leaves.

"Who is Cinthya?"

"The nurse that came in last night and sat with me."

"We don't have anyone on this floor by that name."

"Yes, she's a big lady with an island accent—from the Bahamas or Jamaica. She came last night and sat there on that chair."

"Mildred, we only have three nurses on this wing. Would you like some water?"

"I want Tylenol. I want Morphine. I want the pain to disappear. I want to return to 1987."

She moves around the room, checking everything.

"You will probably be in pain for a while after a spinal tap. I hear they hurt like hell. Your spinal fluid is probably leaking out, and the pressure from it not reaching to your head is causing the pain. I hear it is worse than the worse migraines. Do you feel lots of pressure?"

"Yes."

My eyes are bulging out. Doesn't she notice?

I throw up again. She hands me paper towels. She checks the IV. She checks my pulse. She gets me water. She is there with me, but she's not Cinthya. No matter what she says about not knowing who Cinthya is, I can't shake the late-night interaction I had with that comforting soul. I look at the chair pulled away from the wall.

The phone rings. It stops and rings and stops and rings.

"Do you want me to get it for you?"

"No." I motion with my finger to indicate it's a "definitely no."

She stares at the phone. She wants to answer it.

"Do you want me to call the doctor to see what I can give you for the pain and the nausea?"

"Yes."

I lie flat. I don't want the pillows. I don't want anything but more blankets. I am cold. My blood pressure is low. My heart rate is racing. She leaves. I can't cry. The pain comes back when I cry. I can't talk. I can't sit up.

The nurse comes back and puts something in my IV. She is there. I stare at the chair near the bed again. I think of the beautiful woman who sat with me and inspired me to relax. Soon the painkiller hits me. I am gone.

CHAPTER 7

I awake long after with the man, Jorge, sitting across from me speaking into something black. It looks like a phone. I hear him and I wish he wasn't there. He comes over to the bed. He tries to touch me. I am cold.

"How are you feeling?"

"Like shit." I say between my heavy breaths.

He smiles.

I don't.

"Do you remember anything? Do you remember me now? You ready to come home?"

I understand his Spanish. I shake my head.

"No."

He asks me for the code to retrieve messages from my cellular. I tell him I don't have a cellular, though I smile at the thought of owning one. He shows it to me—a small nearly flat device that looks nothing like the brick-like phones in 1987.

"Can you remember the password?"

"No."

He doesn't understand the word no.

He is perplexed with this answer. He drills me about passwords for the computer. He wants what I can't provide. He wants another woman. He tells me he can't retrieve the business information. He goes into details of accounting. I can't understand it. I don't want to.

He changes the conversation when I close my eyes. I pretend he's not there. I try to hold back the liquid from coming back up.

He tells me that he's brought my oldest son—he was the sixth one, who hadn't come last night. Right now he's downstairs getting breakfast at the cafeteria. I can't open my eyes. The light hurts me.

Jorge tries to sit me up. I motion him away with my arm.

"Don't. I am hurting. Please don't."

"Anyway, your son wanted to see you. If you can't remember, at least pretend. He was at a friend's house last night. He went to school this morning but they called me to pick him up. He was really upset. He's seen you asleep but wants to talk with you."

"Yes."

The boy enters, and for the first time my smile is genuine. I know he's Nathan's son. He's exactly like him, but more handsome. He is his son. The pain disappears for a few seconds. Nate has a son. He's not mine, but he is Nate's.

"Hi, Mom."

"Hi."

"Do you remember me?"

I remember I have to lie.

"A little."

"What happened?"

He comes over and kisses me. He touches my face. He smells of youth. He smells like I smelled two days ago when I was nineteen.

I want to ask him about his dad. I want to know where he is today. I want to hold him and have him here with me.

The boy tells me he is thirteen.

"Do you really remember me, or are you trying to make me feel better?"

"Yes," I lie. "I remember."

"So, you think you are nineteen? I wouldn't be here if you were nineteen."

He laughs then, and I notice he is nervous. He is picking at his thumb nail just like his father. He is twitching and picking at his nail like the day I married his father, and we were waiting to sign the papers, and I held his hand and told him to relax. It was his idea to get married, but he was still a wreck.

I push the bed up to sit. I am in pain. I feel the juices from my stomach fighting for exit. I lie back down. I meet his eyes.

"Are you gonna be okay?"

"Don't know."

I stare into his eyes. I want to cry, but I hold it in.

"When can you come back home?"

"Don't know."

Jorge starts talking to him, and Nate's son, answers him using the word, *Daddy*. I am confused. I lie there, looking at the two of them, at the younger version of Nathan and the man who looks old enough to be my father. His presence makes me nervous. His eyes make me hurt inside. There is a lack of trust from him. I don't know what I know. I don't know, but I know.

The boy's voice brings me back to the moment.

"Mom, do you remember when you ran track in high school?"

"A few years ago."

"No, a long time ago! You always tell me stories of you and when you were growing up. You tell me about your friends. You are a good mom, and so cool. You are one of the coolest moms I know."

I can't grasp the mother comment. I change the subject back to my memories.

To me, high school was two years ago. It was just yesterday.

They both laugh.

"Do you remember 9/11?"

"The emergency numbers? Yeah. We had that back then."

"No, what happened two months ago, on September 11? The

terrorist attacks when tons of people died in New York? You don't remember?"

I scratch my forehead. I hold my head as I shake it.

"No. I don't."

My mother enters. She is worried because I didn't answer the phone after I hung up on her.

"How are you, Millie?"

"Okay."

"You remember Nate? You remember anything about him?"

I nod, yes, then realize she is talking about the boy. I nod again, lying for his sake.

My mother hears, but she never listens.

"Did they give you something for the pain?"

"Yes."

"What did they give you? I bet it was Tylenol 3 with Codeine. Or maybe it is something stronger."

"I don't know."

She starts discussing medicines and about so-and-so who had something done. They did this to them and that to them. I tune her out.

She looks over to the man.

"Jorge, how are you? Did you have any problems getting Nate out of school? Are you on the list at the office? I have never gone to his school so I didn't offer to get him for you. I don't think Millie has me on the emergency contact list."

He nods.

"No problem. Let me get you a chair, Carmen."

"Thank you."

I watch their dance. I watch with pain. I am numb. This is too much. I want everyone out. I want to use the bathroom again, but I don't want to get up. I want to leave, yet I don't. I want to yell and tell them to get out of my face. I want to tell them to look at me and see that I am in pain. I want to grab the two of them and yell to get far away, that I am not who they think I am. Take your shitty conversation somewhere else.

"You haven't eaten your food, Millie."

"Mami, you can have it."

She looks at it and starts to separate the eggs and the toast. She shakes the juice carton. She moves everything and starts dispensing it and giving the bread and jelly to the boy.

He nods no.

She looks at me.

"You want the coffee? Caffeine is good for headaches. I read an article in *Prevention Magazine* that research has shown—"

I interrupt her speech.

"No, you can have it."

The young version of my husband starts to talk. I want everyone out except him. I want to ask about his father. I want to know about his life. I want to know about my life. I want to cross the border to this new reality, to ask how long I've been divorced. I crave to know if he talks with his dad and if his dad misses me. I desire to know what happened to us. I want to, but I don't.

The nurse comes in and tells them that only two people can be here in the room at one time. I stare at her. I am grateful. I owe her bigtime. I think she's an angel.

"We've given her some medication, and she needs to rest. You may wait in the special family room down the hall and take turns to be with her. She had a rough night. She is very emotional."

Jorge tells my mother that she can stay with Nathan.

I only want the boy, but Jorge leaves and doesn't take my mother with him. I close my eyes. She starts on the questions. She starts with the pity. She starts with the shame. She starts with the guilt. She starts. I close my eyes and take deep breaths.

I push the button for the nurse. The young man is worried. He sits at the end of the bed and touches my legs.

"Are you okay, Mom?"

I smile a fake smile and speak.

"Nurse, I need more medicine."

I look at him and tell him that I need to sleep. I am sorry. I can't talk more about high school. I am sorry I don't feel well. I am sorry I don't remember him completely. I lie. I don't remember him at all. I don't remember me. Something tugs inside me. I am breaking into little pieces. Only small parts of me are here.

The nurse comes back in with a syringe and more liquid for my veins. She needs to draw more blood from me. She needs to suck me dry. She signals everyone out, then she leaves, and so do they.

I am alone.

I am sad.

I am scared.

I fall asleep.

CHAPTER 8

It's lunch time. The aide comes in with more food. I wake up to her movements. I ignore her. I don't answer her question about the meals. I pretend to be asleep. She leaves.

I lie staring at the ceiling, trying not to think. The doctor comes in.

"How are you, Millie?"

"Not good."

I start to cry.

"You didn't tell me this was so painful. You just said it would be a bad headache. I suffered from migraines during my high school years and this is worse."

He looks down at me with sympathy.

"I do have good news for you. You don't have meningitis. The test came back negative. How is your memory?"

"The same. I am in a lot of pain."

"I see." But he really doesn't. He shakes his head in agreement with what I am saying.

"Did you move a lot after the procedure? Did you get up?"

"No."

"Well, this is repairable. In a few days you will not have any more headaches. In the meantime, I will make sure you get enough pain medication so you can relax. You need to lie down and just relax." He motions to the TV. "You want me to turn it on for you so you can relax?"

"No. I can't handle the noise."

"Have you eaten anything, Millie?"

"I can't. I can't even look at food."

"Well, you have to try to eat something. It is the only way you can go home. I have to make sure you eat something before I release you tomorrow. Can you promise me that you will eat something today?"

He shakes his head and smiles and I nod yes.

"Anything else you might need?"

"My memory. When will I get my memory back?"

"You should start to remember soon, but there is no time limit on these things. You see, it depends on how long you were unconscious, and we don't know that. No one really can tell these things."

He touches my arm. He has nice warm eyes. He smiles and I know he means what he says. He's just not saying much.

"Okay. I will be releasing you tomorrow if everything goes well."

He is reminding me of the inevitable. I pretend I don't hear.

"Doctor, I need to talk to someone. Is there a psychologist or psychiatrist in this hospital?"

"There is, but he's not here today. I can get his office number and you can set up an appointment with his office in Hollywood."

"No. I need to talk to someone today."

He pulls up a chair, sits and tells me he has good ears. He looks at his watch and tells me he has some time.

"It's okay. I don't feel like I can talk right now. I was just wondering if there was a mental health staff member who would answer questions about a dream I had last night. It shook me up. It's no big deal."

"You've been through a very traumatic experience. You should talk to someone whenever you are ready."

I nod. I agree.

"Very well, Mildred. If you need me, let the nurses know and I will be back in the evening to check up on you. Try to rest."

"Yes. Thank you. Thank you for being so kind."

He stands up and is walking out.

"Doctor, can you do me a favor?"

"Sure. What can I do you for?"

"Can you make sure I don't go home with my mother and the man?"

He smiles and nods his head and leaves.

I know what I know and I know it's not possible.

I fall into a deep sleep.

I have another disturbing dream. I am in Hell. I am knocking on the Devil's door. He doesn't answer. I can hear people screaming. I can smell flesh burning. I can hear torture from inside out and outside in. I can feel it. I keep knocking and hear a voice yell at me to go away, I don't belong there. I am not allowed to enter.

I turn around and see a beautiful angel. She says to come with her. I ask where I am going. She says back to Earth. I tell her no! I don't want to go back there. I want to go to Heaven. She tells me it's not my time. I have too much to live for. I have too much to finish on Earth. I tell her no. I would rather go to Hell. She holds my hand. I can feel her warmth. I can smell her beauty. She smells like a lavender garden. I want to hang on to her. She takes me down a tunnel. I go, I run, and she disappears. I wake up. I am not on Earth. I am back in Hell.

The phone rings and stops. I pick it up. The evening is back. I can see the lights dying down through the blinds.

"Hello."

"Hi, it's me Victoria."

"Hi, Vic."

I begin to cry into the phone. I begin to let it out with the one person I know will hear me. "When are you coming to see me? I have so much to talk to you about. I want you to tell me what is going on."

"I can't tonight and I have to work tomorrow. I will be by this weekend when you get home. Rest. You will see how fast you get your memory back."

"Okay."

"I love you, Millin," she says, using her special name for me.

Vic is the middle sister every family should have. She is an angel.

"Vic."

"Yeah?"

"I miss you."

"Me too. See you soon. Pick up the phone in a little while. Olivia is gonna call you. She tried this morning but no one picked up."

"I had a bad headache. I couldn't answer it."

"Are you better?"

"Some. No, not really. I feel like a Mac truck ran over my body and the tires are still on my head."

"Okay, I love you. Rest, and I'll see you soon."

"Vic?"

"Yes, *mija.*"

"Why is Mami living with me?"

She laughs, hiding something behind the sounds.

"We'll talk soon. I hope you get your memory back. You better do it soon. Bye."

"Goodnight."

I try to get up. I need a shower. I need deodorant. I need clean underwear. I need to brush my teeth. I get up and walk with the IV. I turn my head to one side almost resting on my shoulder. It is better not to hold it all the way straight up. It weighs too much. I can't carry it on my neck. The pain shoots down to my legs, to my pelvis, to my toes. I can't breathe but I make it to the bathroom. I take off the robe. I find the pajamas my mother brought me from the house: her house, their house—not mine.

I turn on the shower, then get in with the IV bag in my hand. The water is hot. It is burning and it feels good. I rest my head underneath the stream. I feel my scalp burning. I feel my eyes resting in my skull in relief. I feel the heat go through and through. It soothes the outside of me. It soothes the inside. I stay there for a while. The bathroom is full of steam. I could sit there under the water forever if this wasn't a hospital. I stand holding the bag, holding on to that soothing feeling for dear life. I know that soon I will have to face the world, a world in which I don't belong.

I get dressed and go back to bed and wait. I wait for something that doesn't seem to come. I wait for God to come down from Heaven. I wait for the angel of death to come get me. I wait for the angel in my dreams to take me back with her. I wait. I wait for what comes over me. Sleep.

I dream I am in a hall when a noise startles me. The noise is loud, as if someone has fallen. I run toward it and push open corridor doors, and that's when I am grabbed and pushed down to the cold floor. I am ripped apart. A man holds me down. A Latin man. A foul-smelling, disgusting, short man. He has a scar across his cheek. He has a knife he places on my stomach and races it up and down to my neck. He wants to fuck me. He wants to fuck me up. He does. His fist is implanted inside my vagina. I get lost in the pain.

I wake up sweating, with my heart rushing up toward my throat. It is racing and I can't catch my breath. I pull the bedpan from underneath the bed and I vomit. I vomit out the man's foul smell. I release the dream. I purge until I can't give more of myself to this world. I vomit because it wasn't just a dream. It was my life at eighteen. It felt like it had just happened. This I remember in small fragments of disgust.

I call the nurse's station. I lie back down on the bed, spent. I am no more. I have no more. The nurse arrives and I'm disappointed to see it's not Cinthya but a woman from the Philippines.

"I can't breathe."

She gets an oxygen mask and places it gently around my face. I breathe in and out. I breathe. She places something in the IV.

I am thankful. In a few minutes I will be gone. Away from here.

CHAPTER 9

It is afternoon. A male nurse is wheeling me to my mother's car. We are going home. Not to my home but to *her* house where she lives with the strange man and six children. I thank the nurse, then I open the white Volkswagen and lay the seat down. I need to lie down. My head can't be held up. I am still weak. My stomach is in one giant knot.

My mother helps me in. I make a comment about her little car. It is a nice new buggy. I hadn't seen anything like it before. She tells me it is fun to drive. She tells me I have one in green. We are out of the parking lot. We are on the street. I break the silence.

"Mami, please don't take me there. Take me to Victoria's house. Take me to Olivia's house. Take me anywhere but there."

"Your niece got married and has a little girl. Did you know this?"

"No." In my mind she is still sixteen.

"Did she call you last night?"

"Maybe. I was sick. I didn't answer the phone. Mom, please, please! Don't make me go there." I beg like a child. I am eight again. I am begging to see my dad. I am begging her to take me to see a man I hardly know. She doesn't because she can't. She has no idea where the man is. My mind drifts to that and then back. I remember the times we saw him and how fast they came and went. I begged for more but rarely got it.

"Mom, please!"

"Millie, you are acting like a child. You will see that once you are home you will start to remember your life. I promise."

"Please don't promise."

"Why? It's the truth. The doctor says you will be better in a few days. The kids can't wait to see you. Jorge is waiting for you. He is a good man. He loves you."

"How old is he?"

"He's fifty."

Fifty! I become silent. He is old, much older than me.

"Now just rest and in a few minutes, we'll be home."

I fight with the liquids in my stomach. I fight to keep them down because I don't want to spoil my mother's new car. I don't want to clean it up after I get out. I don't want to leave anything behind that will remind her of this moment for the rest of her life. I don't want to remember this moment the rest of my life. I don't want this life.

We arrive. It is a gorgeous neighborhood. I sit up and stare at the huge house in front of me. I can't grasp its size. My apartment is small, and in an old area of Hollywood, next to a halfway house. At night you hear the nuts screaming their heads off. You hear the fighting among the drug addicts and the fighting among the ones who think they are Jesus Christ. There are lots of them in there like that. This is not my home, and I would rather hear the screaming of insanity than enter it.

I get out because I need to throw up. I take a few steps and sit on mauve brick pavers in front of the entrance. The door opens and I am bombarded with too much. There are too many faces. I walk in, dragging my heavy head, and lie down in what seems to be a formal living room. I lie down on a very expensive green rug. I am paralyzed. The children run toward me. There are strange faces staring down at a stranger. There is a stranger staring up at them.

I am sick. I can't breathe. My mother gets me a bag. Jorge tells everyone to give me room. This is too much.

Jorge stands above me. "Millie, get up and let me take you upstairs to our room."

Our room. The words shoot through me. They poke me, and tug at me, and make me sicker than I am already.

I don't move. I can't. I am here but I am not. I am me but I am not.

"Millie!"

He bends down to grab me. He tries to hold my heaviness in his arms. This is the first time he has touched me. It is the first time I've allowed him to. He tells the oldest boy to come help him. They drag me up the stairs. I can't focus on the house. I can't focus on anything but getting up the stairs and onto a bed.

I enter a huge room through double doors. It is beautiful. I can see it without having to focus. It is a room I have envisioned in my dreams. The bed is made of light wood and has giant columns on each side. It looks like a room that belonged in Roman times. The woman who decorated it has taste.

I lie down. The man removes my shoes. I place the comforter on top and I close my eyes. This is too much. I open them again and see a huge-screen TV in front of the bed across the room. It looks like a movie theatre. It looks like something out of a magazine.

I close my eyes again, hearing voices. I hear the voices in my head and outside of my head. I hear what I don't want to and what I tell myself. *You will wake up, Millie. This is all a long hellish dream. You will wake up and laugh.*

I am awakened by a little girl standing next to the bed.

"Hi, Mommy!"

"Hi." I gasp for the answer.

"Remember me?"

"Yes." I lie. She's too small to notice.

"I'm Gabriella."

"Beautiful name."

I lie on my side, unable to move my head from the pillow.

"I sleep in here too. Remember?"

"Yes," I lie. She's too small to notice.

"Do you really remember?"

"Yeah, I do." I lie. She's too small but she notices.

"Can I get in bed with you?"

"Not now, please. I have a headache. Go get my mother and tell her I need help getting to the bathroom."

"I'll help you, Mommy."

"No. Go get my mother. Please!"

She leaves running. Her steps on the green tile go through and through my head. I can't breathe. I turn onto my back. It hurts. I am angry and agitated. I am filled with fury and can't let it out. I let the fury take over me and I cry. My mother enters.

"What's wrong?"

"Mom, I can't be here. My heart is racing and I can't catch my breath. I don't fit here. I feel like I am suffocating."

Jorge walks in. He brings me a sandwich. He brings me a soda for my stomach.

"No thanks!"

He insists I eat something. He places the plate on the nightstand. He sits on the bed. My mother leaves to attend to the children's screams. I am not on Earth. I am in Hell.

"How are you feeling? Do you need anything?"

"I feel like shit!"

He smiles. He tries to rub my head. I pull away.

"Don't, please. It hurts."

"Do you want anything at all? Do you want to change into your pajamas?"

"No. I need to go to the bathroom. Where is it?"

He points to the hall in front of the room.

"I can help you. Here, get up."

I move up. I sit up and the muscles in my neck feel as if they are strangling me. I choke and cough and have to lie down again.

"You want me to get a trash can so you can throw up?"

"Yeah."

I breathe in and out slowly.

He brings me rubbing alcohol and a small wash towel. He brings me the trash can. He wets the towel and places it on my forehead. It stings my cut, my bump. I remove it and put it on top of my hair.

"Let me help you again."

We try. I make it up. I get to the bathroom and he waits.

"Can you give me a moment?"

"No, let me stay to help you."

"No. Please leave and close the door."

"But, Millie, I want to make sure you don't fall."

"I won't. Please close the door."

I sit on the toilet and hold my head down against my hands. I can't do this. I can't be here. This is not my home. These are strangers. The house is a museum. I look up at a painting of some naked woman surrounded by angels, in the fucking bathroom. I can't understand who would place a painting of a naked woman in a bathroom. I wipe and get up and flush and wash my hands and open the door. He is still standing there, waiting. He is waiting for a woman who is not there.

He helps me to the bed. I want to sleep.

"What time is it?"

He looks at his watch. "It's six thirty."

"What day is it?"

"It's Friday. It's November 9, 2001."

"And where do I work again?"

"We have a company. We sell industrial parts in Miami. You don't remember?"

"No. Why do I do that?"

"Do what?"

"Sell industrial parts. How did I get into that? I was studying medicine. What happened to that? Did I finish? What happened to my marriage?"

He tries to hold my hand and I move it.

"Do you really not remember anything?"

"Yes, I remember everything," I say sarcastically. "I am faking all this bullshit. I love being part of this drama. I want an Oscar."

"Don't get mean."

"Don't insult me. Forget it. I want to be left alone. Can you leave me alone, sir?"

His smile disappears. He looks angry. He looks frustrated. He looks hurt. His stare penetrates through and through. He's like my mother. He can stare and make me feel like shit. The intimidation suffocates me in a place I cannot understand. What has become of me?

He gets up and leaves. A few minutes later another kid comes running in.

"Please don't run."

"Mom, David hit me."

A little guy jumps on the bed. He hugs me tight. I touch his back.

"Go tell my mother."

Another child comes in.

"Mom, don't listen to him. I didn't hit him. He is such a tattle-teller."

"I am not."

"You are too, Dylan."

"Shut up."

They push each other.

I try to get them to settle down with my words. They don't hear me. I scream. I scream until I have nothing left in my lungs.

"Get out. GET OUT OF HERE! Get out of this room! Get out,

both of you. Go somewhere else."

They stare at me, motionless. They are in shock. I don't move. I just stare at them.

My mother comes through the door, telling them to go, to leave me alone, and to go eat dinner. I hear Jorge screaming at them in Spanish with a stern voice that shakes me. I feel bad that they are in trouble. I feel bad that I am here. My mother asks if I need the medication she got from the hospital.

"Yes."

"Okay, I'll be back."

I hear her yelling downstairs.

Nathan walks in. Not my husband, the younger version from the hospital. "Hi, Mom."

He lies next to me.

I am dumbfounded by how no one listens to anyone in this place.

"Mom, how are you feeling?"

"I am sick."

"You know, Craig wants to come over but Daddy and Momo won't let him."

"Who's Craig?"

"My best friend. He's practically part of the family. He lives down the street. Once you see him, you'll remember him."

"Aha." I let out air from my mouth. He looks at me and continues.

"Well, can he come over? He wants to see you."

"Go ask Jorge."

"He said no."

"Then I guess there is your answer."

I am exasperated. I am exhausted. I want the pills and I want to sleep.

He gets up and mumbles something on the way out.

I am not fit for this. I want silence. I want to be left alone. I want out of this parallel dimension that has me paying for some screwed-up karmic debt I've done there.

I turn over on my side and my eyes catch a frame on the nightstand. I bring it close to me. It is me. I am young. A younger version of Jorge is sitting next to me. His hair is dark. I look like myself. We are dressed in fancy clothes. I trace the picture with my finger. Where was I? When was this picture taken? Who are you? The picture is silent. My mind is too. I place it back and my mother brings me the pills.

"You are supposed to take these with food."

"Mom, I'll eat later."

"No, you must eat before you take them."

"Mom, give me the pills." I pop them both and swallow. I give her back the water.

"Okay, I will be downstairs. I will make sure the kids don't come up. Rafaela will be in tomorrow morning. I asked her to come help me with the kids. She left early this afternoon. You'll have to pay her extra for Saturday. Maybe she can come Sunday too."

"Who's Rafaela?"

"The Colombian woman you met at the hospital. She takes care of the house and the kids after school."

"She's a nanny."

"Yeah, but don't call her that."

"What?"

"Never mind." She leaves.

I find comfort in the discomfort. I am alone. I am warm but I am not home. I sleep.

CHAPTER 10

I am awakened by the little girl moving on the bed at the far corner of the room behind a desk. She's moving her head from side to side and sucking on her thumb. She does this is at a speed that would give anyone a headache. She is falling asleep, and I try not to disturb her as I get up and slip from the room.

It's a small victory when I find my way back to the bathroom. I walk to the sink, refusing to look at the mirror. I do not want to see that woman again—the one with the messed-up hair, is carrying extra weight, and has bags under her eyes. The one who doesn't smile.

All I want right now is to brush the taste of rotten liquid from my mouth. I see several toothbrushes and grab the red one. I don't care. I stare at a huge tub. I look to the left to the shower. I want a shower. I want to stand in the heat and let it take me. I get undressed. I turn on the water and get in. It should have occurred to me to lock the door, but it didn't.

I jump when the man walks in. "You need anything?"

"Get out," I say, grabbing a towel to cover myself, "Get out of here!"

He comes closer. "Millie, I've seen you naked hundreds of times."

"No! Leave!"

"Millie, come on. Please!"

I yell. I cry. I hang on to the towel with my fists.

"Get out of here!"

He does.

I sit on the tile and cry.

I let the water wash me down. I am grossed out. I am disgusted. My head is splitting in two. It will bleed soon. It will open up and my brain will wash down the drain. It will. I can feel it, ready to break.

I get up and wash off the soap, then grab the towel again to start drying myself. Fresh tears erupt when I realize I didn't bring clothes with me. I don't want to go out there with him. I don't want to walk out of here undressed. I want clothes. I want Nate. I want my home. I want my little bathroom in our one-room apartment. I want me at nineteen. I want to experience and remember what I can't. I let the tears and the sounds come out. I don't hold back. I hold onto the towel more tightly. I feel the expansion of my heart pumping blood everywhere but to my brain. I can feel the restriction of memories pulsating up there without release.

After a while he knocks on the door. "You okay in there?"

I don't answer.

"Millie, are you okay?"

"Yeahhhhh."

I lie. I lie so he doesn't ask anymore.

Relief washes over me when I spot a large green robe on a hook and put it on. As I do so, I'm careful to avoid contact with the woman in the mirror. She's not me. I am not her.

When I get to the room, he is not in there, just the little girl. She is sleeping. She is beautiful. I had noticed her green eyes that afternoon, and they were like none other I have ever seen. She's not mine.

I go to the dresser. I open up one drawer, then another and another. I need underwear. I need pajamas. I need socks. I need my memory. I find everything in different drawers. Messy drawers. Men's drawers. I find kinky underwear and bras. I find huge boxers. I find clothes

I wouldn't be caught dead in. I find nothing reminiscent of me. I can't find myself in these drawers. I find a book and open it to see my own handwriting. It has pictures cut out from magazines and pasted on pages with notes written around them. It has poetry, also in my handwriting. It has sketches. It has words that were written by my hand yet they are not mine. I begin to read a passage and the sadness from each sentence forces me to close it. I want to continue reading it, but I don't. I can't. This is someone's private thoughts. My head spins at thoughts of entering someone else's place in this world. It spins and spins and spins until I can't think. These thoughts come in and out as fast as I place the journal back under the clothes. This woman is insane to live like this.

I get dressed with what I can find and slip back into bed. Jorge comes in, wearing boxers and a t-shirt.

"Where do you think you are going?" I ask as he approaches the bed.

"I sleep here."

"Not tonight. Not with me."

"Millie, come on. I won't touch you. It's late and I need to get up early to go to the ranch."

"You are not sleeping in here."

"Millie!"

He is pissed. I can see it on his face. I can hear it in his voice. I can sense it in his gestures. He is tired, but not nearly as tired as me.

"Okay, I will sleep on this side and I promise I won't move."

I place all the pillows and cushions in between us. I make a wall.

"If you move over these pillows I will scream. The little girl will wake up. My mother will wake up. I will make sure the entire house wakes up. You put a bloody foot over this and so help me God, I will lose it."

"Okay, Millie. Whatever you want!" He pauses. "Goodnight. I hope you feel better."

I don't answer. I try to find comfort in the discomfort. I can't. I barely sleep throughout the night. I stare at the ceiling and watch for lights from passing cars. I try to distinguish the noises from the neighborhood. I can hear the little girl's snore. I can hear his heavy breathing. I lie still, waiting for my mind to go back into place. I wait. I wait but it doesn't go back. I try to recall the last memory or the first memory of anything in this life.

I think of two weeks prior to this fiasco of a life. I think about Nate's mini getaway. I think about making love to Nate under the moonlight and how romantic he was that night. How we celebrated his twentieth birthday back in 1987. I think about the roller coaster ride at Busch Gardens and how I couldn't get enough. I think and think and think, and wait and wait. He is not here. He is somewhere and can't find me. I don't know if he will ever find me again. I don't know if I will ever find myself again. I begin to cry. It is a soft cry because I don't want to wake anyone, but it comes from deep inside the hollow piece of space inside my chest. I try to find the strength to believe there is a reason for all this. I think of the nurse, Cinthya, and the words she had spoken to me that night: "You know that everything has a divine purpose. I can bet that years from now you will see this moment as a pivotal wake-up call of sorts."

With sleep nowhere in sight, I start to converse with God. When I get no answers, I sit in my silence and wait for a miracle or a sign of some sort. I only hear snores and heavy breathing. I am here but I am not. A part of me has died or at least it's missing. God knows this. Maybe I am never supposed to remember. Maybe there is a purpose in this. Suddenly, my sadness turns to anger. Anger at God for not returning my memory. I lie there, continuing to push Him for answers that don't come.

The pain begins once more. Is it His wrath? I am afraid. I am sorry. I didn't mean what I said. I didn't mean what I thought. Wouldn't it be better if I were dead? Death, I can handle right now.

It would be no different from this. Eventually I find sleep, but not for long.

When I next open my eyes it is morning. The little girl has left and so, thankfully, has the man. I feel the heaviness of the pressure inside my head. It reminds that I am here, but not.

I get up and go toward the closets. I open the right one and go in. It is full, but has nothing for me.

Nate comes in. Every time I see him, I see his father. I see what I remember. I see what I no longer have.

"Mom, what are you looking for?"

"Clothes!"

"That's not your closet. That's Daddy's. Your closet is the other one."

I walk out and open the other one. It is larger. It is a closet full of too much. It has women's clothes but also has nothing for me.

"Mom, you need help?"

"No."

I sit on the floor in the middle of the closet. I stare at the shoes. I stare at the clothes. I stare at the sizes. I have gained at least thirty pounds. Clothes are no longer Madonna and the eighties are definitely gone. It is someone else's style.

"Mom, are you okay?"

"Yeah."

"You need help getting up?"

"No."

I am numb. Even getting dressed has become an obstacle. I lie on the cold tile. I place a blanket under my head. He stares at me and comes down to sit.

"Mom, is it really that bad?"

I let the tears fall out. It is. I don't say it, but it is.

He reaches for my shoulder. He places a warm hand on it. He is assuring me that I will be fine.

"How do you know?"

He laughs. He smirks. "Because it will be."

He tells me a bit about my life and my hobbies. It is the lack of certain hobbies that stands out to me.

"Nate, do I really not paint?"

"Not anymore."

The tears flow. I let them go.

"What happened to your dad?"

"You broke up. He got remarried and I think had another kid. I don't know."

"Do you see him?"

"Nope. Not since I was three."

"And how am I dealing with this? How do I deal with so many kids?"

He brings his knees toward his chest. "You do. I don't know how, but you do. Some days you go crazy but you just get through them. You have a way of making everyone's life easy. I don't know what you do when we aren't around."

I look up at him.

"Can you help me up and help me find something remotely interesting to wear? My sister is coming over."

He helps. He says something funny. I laugh. We laugh. I am instantly reminded that my head needs to rest. I can't hold it up. I can't look up. I go to the bathroom and get dressed. I use someone else's toothbrush. I stare in the mirror and fix the hair. I am really not her. I am just her body's temporary tenant. I am keeping it warm for her until she returns.

I get ready to enter another day. I sit on the side of the tub. I try to gather up courage to go downstairs while pushing the tears away. I am alone without a memory and yet so much haunts me. The house haunts me. The children haunt me. The man haunts me. My grandparents haunt me. My mother haunts me. I am haunted by what I can't recall. I am erased little by little while barely holding on.

As I leave the room, I notice a painting on the top of the headboard. It is of a woman lying on her stomach looking out at the audience. She's in an orange gown. The picture is old. It stops me. She is not of this time. She is not, but the emptiness in her eyes is. Her seriousness is seductive. I kneel on the end of the bed and stare. We stare at each other. I am her. I am not but I am. It is the only thing here that makes sense. She is a small piece of my puzzle, her eyes searching for answers across the cement. She is searching and I am here. She's not alone. I am brought back to now.

My sister is downstairs. I can hear her voice. I walk slowly holding my head to one side. There is my sister. Like me, she's heavier and looks much older, but I can still recognize the gorgeous woman I remember from my teenage years. My sister is fifteen years older than me but at this moment she is even more so.

"Vic, how are you?" I kiss her and hug her.

"Millie, how you feeling?"

"Like shit."

She laughs and hugs me back.

My mother motions us to sit on the sofa. Kids are eating and watching cartoons. Kids are everywhere. I take a look at the house. It is not me. My mother offers me something to eat. I tell her that I would like some cereal. I would get it myself but I can't find my way in any part of this house. She says fine. I hear all their voices at once. They muffle through me. This is a house full of people. This is a house without silence. This is not my house.

We eat and then I go back upstairs to bed. My sister lies next to me. It's mid-morning. The kids are off with the Colombian woman. She's taken them to a park. There is silence.

"Where's Carlos?"

"Carlos and I are divorced."

"What? Why?"

She laughs. She tells me it was a long time coming. They were never a match. But she still cares for him deeply and sees him often. She lives alone in my mother's old apartment. The apartment I grew up in, the apartment near my home with Nate and another life.

I stare at Vic, noting how much older she looks. It is as disconcerting as my own reflection.

"So how do you feel today?"

"So-so. I can't get rid of the headaches. It feels like someone is stabbing me in the neck and not letting me keep the blood flowing to the top of my head."

"Yikes. That hurts!"

"Yeah. And, Vic, why is Mami living with me?"

"You asked her to move in with you and Jorge. You are building a huge house on many acres and she will be living there."

I cannot relate to this.

"What happened to me and Nathan?"

"I really don't know the entire story. I think it was he cheated on you while you were pregnant with David."

I always love stories. I love novels. This is a story. She is telling me a story about me, but it's not me. I lie there holding her arm. I love my sister more than anything. Today I find that the motherly bond she has for me is stronger. She is not telling me the entire truth. She is holding back. She doesn't want to hurt me. But I ask for more. I want more, and I need it.

"What do you mean he cheated on me?"

"I really don't know." She stares at the ceiling fan. She changes the subject. She wants to know how I am feeling.

"Vic, please don't do this." I hold her tighter. I lie there on that king-sized pillow, holding in my heart. It is breaking slowly. I cannot keep the pieces together.

"Tell me the truth."

"I promise, I am telling you what I know. You really never told anyone the details of why you left him. He gave you a horrible time in the divorce. He has never paid child support and hasn't seen the boys in eleven years. David never met him. He was just a few months old. You met Jorge, I think, in December and by January you had left Nate. He helped you out tremendously. He got you an apartment and has been a father to all the kids."

I don't want to hear this. No—I do want to hear it, but I don't want to accept it as my life.

"What can I possibly have in common with him?"

"I don't know."

She looks over at me as tears trickle down the sides of my face onto the pillow.

"Millie, don't cry. I really don't want to talk about this. You will get your memory back and figure all this out on your own. Please don't ask me anything."

I stay silent. I stay crying. I keep my breathing slow. I want my heart to stay inside. I want my head to stay in one piece. I want to stay. I want to go. I want it all gone. She changes the subject.

"Did you speak with Olivia?"

"Yeah. She told me about her little girl. How does it feel to be a grandmother?"

"Old."

"You aren't old. Hey, if I am nineteen then you are thirty-four."

"I wish, Mija."

She laughs. I smile. I wipe the tears. I cannot wipe my heart. I feel comfort in this discomfort. I am not alone. I am only alone in my thoughts. I think about sharing my dream with her—the one of the scar-faced man—but I don't. I am on sensory overload. I hear the kids are back and my mother starts yelling.

"I don't remember Mami ever yelling like this before."

Vic laughs. "She never had to deal with this many kids!"

"Those aren't children. They are spawns of the devil. They are wild and untamed. They aren't human. They are out of control. How can I deal with this every day?"

She laughs again and tugs at me, making me smile.

"I couldn't be responsible for raising them. I would have to be out of my mind."

"You are!"

"You think?"

"Hey, you got them. We thought you were crazy but you manage to keep them in a sane atmosphere. You give them the love they have needed and they listen and love you for it."

"Why would I adopt four kids?"

"That's a funny story."

She looks at me again. She turns to her side and props up on her elbow. I watch every movement, breathing in its familiarity.

"You had your tubes tied the day after David was born."

"So, I can't have any kids?"

"You want more than this?"

"No, no, no!" I shake my head but I shouldn't. It hurts.

"No, what I mean is I will never have anymore?"

"Not unless there is a miracle. Jorge is fixed too. He has three grown kids from two other marriages."

"Why aren't we married?"

"Don't really know. I think you should ask him that."

"Why would I go to Romania to adopt them?"

"Oh, you didn't! The agency brought them to you at the Ft. Lauderdale Airport. Gabriella came on the day of your thirtieth birthday."

"Have I really lost my mind?"

She laughs. We lay there listening to the yelling downstairs.

"How's my dad?"

She is silent.

"How is my relationship with him?"

"Your dad passed away not long ago. You hadn't spoken to him in years because he lost his memory. He got really sick. I think it was cancer. He didn't remember anyone. He was really old. You went to Puerto Rico to see him a few years ago and made your peace with him. You also cleared things with his wife. It really wasn't for you to ask forgiveness for whatever happened between him and Mami. But, in your Millie fashion of clearing karma, you did your best to bring peace to his wife."

I cry. I cry because I remember seeing him at eighteen, right after I left home. It didn't go well. It didn't go well at all. It was last year in my memory bank.

I don't need to comment—Vic understands because her father died when she was in her twenties.

We talk a little more and then she tells me she needs to go. I beg her not to.

"I have to, Millie."

"I love you."

"Me too."

I get up with her to go downstairs and find the nanny making lunch. The kids are watching television and I sit in the midst of the chaos. I lie down on the sofa. I see a dog in the backyard. A huge black dog, German Shepherd.

"She's not yours, is she?"

Micaela, the oldest girl answers, yes.

They let the dog in.

I jump. I am afraid of dogs. Ever since my oldest sister's mutt bit me as a teenager I have been afraid of them.

The dog runs towards me, wagging her huge tail. I feel my heart wanting to come out. I feel sick.

"Mama, get down!" David calls to her.

"Her name is Mama?"

"Yeah, like Big Mama. Don't be afraid, Mom. She's your dog.

You found her and she's been with you for many years."

"I have never been a dog person. I am a cat person."

"Well, you have a cat here too. He's hiding."

I lie back. I am hiding too. Somewhere inside there is me and the me outside is not the same. I am hiding. I am lost. I cannot find my way back.

CHAPTER 11

As the day progresses, I sit with my mother. I want to talk without causing a fight.

"Where are my friends? Do I have any of the same friends from high school?"

"I guess you do. I really don't know. I know you have Lisa."

"Who's Lisa?"

"Your massage therapist. You two are very close."

I watch her as she folds the laundry. I watch her carefully.

"Can you call her? Does she know what has happened to me?"

"I don't know. I don't have her number. It's not like I have your friends' numbers."

I lie back down on the sofa. I lay the blanket on me. I am beginning to feel self-pity overtake me—which is unlike me. I never feel sorry for myself. There is no connection to anything in this house. There is no link to my past. There is no attachment to who I am. I have skipped over everything. There are chapters missing in a book. I started fine in the beginning, skipped over the middle, and found the last page. What has happened in between?

Jorge comes in and says he is going back to "the ranch," as he calls it.

"You want to come and see where you will be living in a few weeks?"

"No."

"You should go, Millie. You will love it. You already love it."
My mother pushes. He pulls. It is a tug of war.

"I'll go."

We get in the car. I have to lie down. I cannot keep my head up
too long. Nausea and pain fill me if I stand up too long. I don't see
where we go. I don't hear anything he says. I don't care.

"Can you at least try to talk to me?"

I ignore him.

We arrive at the place. I get out and stare at it. It is a ranch-style
home. There is not much to see. It is being finished. There is nothing
elaborate about the architecture. The house where I am staying is
nicer. There is a great amount of land. It has a large pond next to
the house. It seems peaceful. It seems miles away from the world.

"Come in?" He says like a question as he opens the front door.

There are men working on the floors. There are men hammering
away and talking and smoking. I am sick. The noises go through
and through. I walk through the entrance and find the exit across
the house. I vomit on the grass. I lie on the grass. Jorge gets me up.

"Come. Sit in the terrace. There is a large swing you can sit on."

I let him help me. I let him touch me and guide me to the terrace.
I let him guide me in this life I have forgotten, erased in a way that
now fits but causes fear.

I sit down and he sits next to me. He tries to push the swing
with his legs.

"Please don't."

"Sorry." He pauses. "Do you like the house?"

"I haven't seen it. It seems nice. I really don't care right now."

Tears swell up and I let them. I let them flow through me and
out of me.

"Why are you crying?"

"I don't deserve all this."

"Why? Have you done something that makes you feel you are unworthy?"

"Why would you ask that? Why would you ask me if I've done something? I just don't fit in this life. We have money. I had none before. We have nice cars and fancy houses. I had a one-bedroom apartment in the middle of a shitty neighborhood. I don't deserve this."

He tries to hold me. I pull away.

"Please don't."

"Do you really not remember me?"

I ignore the stupid question and place my head in my hands. My face stares at my lap. The inside of my palms feels like sand. I am still mangled. I am damaged goods. I know this. I am aware of a foul smell that comes up from my soul. I don't know why, but it's there. I live within it.

"I can't do this. Please take me back to my mother's."

"Millie, give it time. I am sorry."

"Sorry for what, Jorge?"

"Sorry for making you suffer so much. We've had a tough year. I've put you through so much."

"I don't understand."

"There is a lot you don't know."

"I don't want to know. Jorge, save the confessions for when, and if, I get my memory back. Please don't say anything that I will remember later on as being new. I will get angry then and have to carry it everywhere. I can't handle any more stories. I can't handle any more fucking shit. I can't handle the pain in my head, the nausea in my stomach, and this so-called miserable life that, apparently, I've created while forgetting my dreams."

He stops. He stops his legs and his gestures. He stops and waits for me. He is waiting for me to continue. He wants forgiveness for what I cannot forgive at this moment. I don't know who he is. I can't grasp at this lifeline. I have questions. I have a lot of them. I have no energy to ask. I really don't want to know. How did I get from there to here? How is it that a thirty-three-year-old woman can forget fourteen years of her life? How is it that I haven't accomplished any of my dreams? I had a lot of them, and they're gone. I realize I will not have Nathan. I will not have my apartment. I will not have that life. I realize I don't paint anymore. I haven't painted in years. I asked my oldest son. *My oldest son!* The thought of him being my son is surreal. The fact that they are all my children is too much. He told me I swore I would never paint again. I don't do anything but work and take care of children. This is not a life for anyone.

I get up. I fall back down. I cry. Jorge tries again to hold me. I let him. His arms wrap around me like a warm jacket. His smell falls on my skin. I want to pull away. I want to stay away from this stranger. I want to find my way back. If this is who I am I want to know that I am happy here. I want to know that all these years have had meaning for me. I pull away. I wipe my tears. I blow my nose with the bottom of my shirt. He laughs. He says something funny in Spanish and I laugh. It hurts. It hurts to let go and it hurts to hold on. I want to say goodbye to my grandparents. I want to say goodbye to my father. I want to say goodbye to Nathan. I want to say goodbye to me.

"Do you love me? Do I love you?"

He stares at me.

"Do you?"

"I never say it, but I do."

"You never say it?" I can't understand the answer.

He nods no.

"Why are we together and for so long?"

"Because we are the same."

"We are not the same."

"We are, Millie. We are the same. We are very different but we are the same. Give it time and you will see that everything I do is for you and the kids. I have screwed up so much in my life and this accident, or whatever it is, has cleared up some stuff. I need you. I can't run the business without you. I can't take care of these kids without you. I am nothing without you and you are nothing without me."

I listen, but can't relate. I can't relate to this need…to all of his needs. I want to understand. I want to, but I am too far away.

We stop moving. I stop asking. He stops telling. I sit there, letting pity take over again. I sit there with someone, but I am alone. I hold onto the swing. I hold onto the little bit of me. It's a bumpy ride. This is all a bumpy ride. We sit for a while until the nausea leaves. I watch the horses across the pool, I watch the chickens and all the trees. I watch a life that isn't mine and can't understand the added responsibility of taking care of another when I can't find me right now.

We stand together and walk back through the house. He shows me around. It will be nice, eventually. I tell him this and he feels proud. He has designed a lot of it. He says it's been two years of trial and error. He tells me we have a lot of financial problems. We've lost a lot of money. We've lost everything but this house. He tells me little details I can't understand and don't care to. He doesn't want to burden me anymore with it. I thank him. I really don't care right now. I want to go lie down.

CHAPTER 12

We leave it all behind. I leave the uneasiness of him. I leave what will not be mine if I can wake from this dream. I will go back to my simple life. I will go back to loving endlessly and trying to turn a bad boy into a good one. I want to know I can change him and have a long life ahead. I don't want this pitstop. I don't want this dead end. I don't want this life. We leave.

We turn into the main road towards the other house. I see something familiar. It is the park from that night. I tell him. I tell him what I know, slowly. He asks if I want to enter it.

"No. I don't care to."

"Are you sure? Maybe it will trigger something?"

"No, I am sure. I want to go lie down. Seeing it won't fix anything."

"Okay."

"This is a safe neighborhood so I don't think anything really bad could've happened to you."

"It already has."

We enter Hell's quarters again. The kids are playing some computer games. I head to the bedroom. He follows. I let him.

I lie down and he sits on the bed. He wants to talk. He is nervous. He wants things the way they were with the woman he loves.

"Do you know what happened that night you had the accident?

I mean, do you want to know?"

"No."

He continues anyway. "We had an argument. We have been having lots of them lately. I had too much to drink at the ranch with the workers. It was my fault."

His eyes begin to water and he turns away.

"Jorge, I really don't want to know. It doesn't matter to me. Anything you tell me right now will seem like a story about another person. It isn't about me. It is about a woman who is not here right now. Give it time. That's what everyone keeps telling me. You will make me sicker than I feel right now. I have too much anger for being here. Please. Don't add to this nightmare!"

I want to touch him. I don't. He is not my husband. A large part of me is scared of him.

"Do you forgive me?"

"I have nothing to forgive. I don't know what it is I am supposed to forgive you for."

"I've hurt you so much. I am sorry. I don't ever say that I'm sorry, but I am really sorry. I have done so many stupid things. I have accused you of so many stupid things because of my jealousies. I am very insecure about us. The ranch has taken so much of my time and I've neglected the business. I've neglected you. I accused you of so much. I don't know if it's true or just my imagination."

I interrupt him. I feel like I am being drilled. I am scared and uncomfortable with this conversation, with this man.

"Do we normally get along?"

"Yes. I was a married man when we met."

"I really don't want to know anymore."

"But let me continue."

"No." I say, shaking my head over and over. "No. Please. I need silence. Look at my eyes. They are bulging out. They are carrying a world that's already too heavy."

"You are a very stubborn woman and I have to constantly go around that."

I smile. He is telling me the truth. Some things never change. Stubbornness is not a good quality in me. I know. I tell him I know. I tell him to please let me sleep. I ask him to bring me some of the painkillers.

"You need to eat something."

"I did and I threw it up."

"Yeah, but you still need something in your stomach or the pills will burn it."

It is already burned. I am burned and so is my head. My freaking head is ashes. I think this but I don't say it. I hear my brain yelling it, but it doesn't come out. The thoughts pound through the bumps, bruises, and scratches.

"I will eat later. Just get me the pills, please."

"Okay. But can we talk later tonight?"

He rubs my head. I let him but I don't want to.

"I guess."

"Can we go for a walk?"

"I can't, Jorge. I can barely stand."

"Well, then we can go back to the ranch and sit and talk."

"Maybe. We'll see. Okay?"

He brings me back a soda and the pills. I swallow hard and tears come again. I don't know why they've appeared again. I don't know. I don't.

I find the remote control to the giant television and I turn it on. There are hundreds of channels and nothing I want to watch. There is lots of news about 9/11. I still don't understand what has happened as I watch a story about the event. I begin to cry.

There is a reason for everything, but it is difficult to comprehend what has happened in New York. I don't grasp the story. I don't understand the details. It is not about me, yet it is. It is about people who cannot be forgotten. It is about people who will never be able to remember again. It is a little bit of my drama. I turn it off. This is too much right now. It is not 1987. It is not October. It is not my life. It is not their life.

I am here.

I am not.

CHAPTER 13

It's Sunday. I have noticed one of the middle girls doesn't talk much. She is there but she's not. I question my mother.

"She's mentally handicapped."

"What?"

"She's a little slow. You got her when she was nine years old—she's eleven now—and you didn't know this at the time. The adoption agency misguided you. She is not easy. It is a struggle for you every day. I can't handle her. I am afraid of that child."

"What? I don't understand what you are telling me...."

"What don't you understand?" She sits next to me at the kitchen table. "What is so hard for you to understand?"

"I have a mentally challenged child in this house? I have six children. I understand some have learning disabilities and now you are telling me that this child is not all there? Anything else you want to share?"

"She has to be injected with growth hormones every day. She hasn't gotten her shots since you had the accident."

"I inject what?"

She goes into the refrigerator and pulls out a bag with medication.

"She has to be injected every day with this. I don't know how to use the syringe pen so she hasn't received her shots."

"Does she know how to do it herself?"

"No."

"I don't understand. What is all this?"

I drop the bag with the medicine and push it toward her. I cannot listen to this. I don't know how I can live like this. I don't know why I would bother to get up each morning and do this every day. I say nothing. There is nothing to say.

"Millie."

She takes a deep breath. "Millie, this is your life. This is not a life I would have wanted for you. This is the life you've made for yourself. I know it's hard and I know it seems to be difficult right now, but you do what you need to do every day. I don't know how or why you would want this, but this is it. I pray for you every day to give you strength."

She goes and grabs a calendar agenda with the week written out. There are therapist appointments, doctor appointments, extracurricular events, teacher meetings, and so much more that I am dizzy from just reading the week ahead. I fall silent, feeling fury running through me like a freight train. I cannot pick any words that will not insult her because I want to take it out on someone. I can't find eloquence right now to tell her that she did not make it easy for me growing up. This is not a piece of cake, but neither was living as a teenager with her. She has somehow forgotten the details. I am not going to remind her. I am beyond this. I just sit.

"Are you okay?"

"Yes, Mom! No! I am not okay. Is there someone that I see? Is there a therapist I visit, with all this drama in my life? I mean, I can't imagine that I don't have a nervous breakdown once a week. It's no wonder I am overweight and look like an old woman. I live for every goddamn person in this house but me. No wonder I lost my memory. I think God is giving me a break. He has decided to place me on a mental vacation. I should be thanking Him instead of cursing at Him."

82

She has ignored my rant and is staring outside the window thinking. "I think you go see someone but I really don't know."

"Do I have an address book anywhere in this house, or is this agenda the only form of my schedule and existence?"

"I don't know. I have no idea where your things are. If you haven't noticed, most of the things are packed so we can move in two weeks. I moved last month and everything is in the garage."

I want to ask her how is it possible that she doesn't know where my things are. It was always her business to know everything. I want to tell her I am still angry for what I believe was last year. I want to make her apologize for the humiliations with Nathan. I want her to tell me she is really sorry. But there is no more Nate. There are fourteen years in between now and last year. There are pregnancies, a divorce, and adoptions in between then and now. There are new neighborhoods, new cars, different careers, and a different mate. There is too much in between then and now. Since I cannot bring myself to start, much less finish, I just sit holding my head and pulling my hair to get the blood flowing. It no longer seems to flow to my brain, as if the top portion of me has been erased: as if, little by little, my whole self is being erased.

"You want to eat anything?"

"No, thanks."

"I finally called Lisa and she's coming to see you today."

"Who?"

"Your friend Lisa. The massage therapist I told you about. Jorge had her number. She used to massage him too."

"Ah, yeah, right."

"She'll be here around noon. She was very concerned about your accident. She's a nice lady."

"Mom, where is the rest of our family? My oldest sister has called, but hasn't come by. Olivia and her family are nowhere in sight. I mean, where is the rest of this family?"

"Everyone is busy."

I want to tell her that things never change. I got married at a courthouse at eighteen. I had no family there. No one wanted any part of my union with Nathan. That was an excuse then. Now, everyone is busy. I ran away from my home life just to end up right back living the same. Things never change.

"Mom, what happens if I don't get my memory back?"

"Please don't even mention that. I am seventy-seven years old. I cannot raise your children. I am through raising children." She smiles. There is honesty in her sarcasm. She is joking, but she is not. I understand this and I don't blame her. This house is chaotic. I am a large part of the chaos. I am in the center of it all. She raised me alone. She helped raise Olivia when Victoria divorced the first time. This is who she is. She is strong. Even in her older years she is strong. I know my mother loves me. I know her obsessive compulsiveness drives her crazy. I know this, but I can't acknowledge it to her. I am quiet. I share, but I don't. I stay within my boundaries and pray she stays in hers.

CHAPTER 14

Shortly past noon, two women enter the house. They kiss my mother and they come toward the sofa.

"Hi, Millie."

"Hi."

They each give me hugs and kisses. I don't know them. I don't know who and what they want. My mother introduces them.

"This is Lisa and Monique."

"Hi."

"Monique is a doctor. Lisa is your massage therapist. They are close friends of yours."

"Hi."

I can't break the ice. I can't, but I try.

They sit on the sofa and each child comes to kiss them. They are well behaved. They are nothing like they were an hour ago. I am stunned.

Lisa touches my hand and stares into my eyes.

"How are you feeling?"

"Ah, well, with a nice headache, but I'm here."

"What happened to you?"

"I don't know."

I tell her part of the story, the quick version. It's too long and I am too drained to relive it. It comes out like water without shape.

It comes out with heat from overexposed coals full of fury.

Monique is concerned that the headaches have been going on for too long. She knows of the effects of a spinal tap, and it's been too many days. She suggests I go back to the doctor. She mentions an epidural blood patch to seal the leakage and that it must be done in the hospital. She tries to explain that it is painful but it will relieve the headache in time; otherwise, this healing can take very long and the headaches will continue. I listen attentively while thinking of more pain, as if there could actually be any more pain coming out of me.

She stays to talk with my mother while Lisa tells me to go outside with her to talk.

I follow and we sit on a bench in the terrace. I don't know her. I don't know what it is that feels good about her. She's a stranger but her hug, and her warmth, engulfs me without fears. I open up. I tell her my life as I know it. I tell her about Nathan and it's new to her. I tell her things that apparently the other woman, the other Millie, never mentioned. I tell her I am intimidated by Jorge.

She tells me she likes him but she knows that we have our differences.

I tell her I don't understand what has become of me.

She tells me what everyone tells me. *Rest and it will come. Give it time.*

I am tired of giving it time. I am tired of giving into time. I know. She knows. I wonder what else she knows. I wonder how well she knows me. I wonder what I am doing pouring out my soul to a stranger.

She laughs.

She knows me very well. She tells me I am a very stubborn woman. She tells me I called her a week or so before, and told her I was going to kill myself.

I ask why. I am unable to fathom this.

"You called me up crying one evening and told me that you

almost killed yourself. You'd had enough. You'd lost everything. You'd lost millions of dollars. Your business is falling apart. You owe so much money that you feel you cannot pick up the pieces. The calls from credit companies, customers, and factories are too much, and it's all on you because you are the one who runs the company. Your pride is in the way and you can't accept the feeling of failure. You can't handle the kids. Your relationship with Jorge is the worst it's ever been."

I interrupt. "Lisa, do I want to know this?"

"You should. It's who you are. You told me you drove by an overpass several times in the middle of traffic. You hesitated and did not drive off the bridge. You got off at the next exit and drove back again. Each time you didn't think of you but of an innocent person you would kill when the car landed in the middle of rush hour. You called me crying and told me that you couldn't take it. This was shit. This life was shit."

"I believe it. I can see it. No wonder I lost my memory."

She laughs. She holds me.

I start to cry, softly. They are tears of frustration, tears of bottled-up anger. They are tears of the unknown. This is a horrible story. This is all a horrible life.

"Millie, I don't know how you will come out of this. I don't know what happened to you a few nights ago in the park. I don't even know what the fuck you were doing there so late. I do know that you needed to get some sense knocked into you. You were falling into a black hole. I was worried. Monique and I have been deeply worried about you. You are a stubborn knucklehead. You are just too proud to ask for help. I can't tell you how I pray for a light to shine upon you. Well, maybe this is a blessing."

In that moment I remember Cinthya saying, *"Nothing goes unnoticed in your life. These are the events that mold you, make you, and force you to evolve to a higher spiritual level. Maybe you've been praying for a break in this life. And, here it is. You don't know until you know."*

I look up at her with the pain going through and through. "I don't think so."

"Tell me what you know."

"Nothing. I don't know shit. I don't know what I am supposed to do with this crap. What if I don't get my memory back? What am I supposed to do without those years?"

"You make new ones. Hell, I don't think this happened without a good reason. This was a stop. You were in bad shape. You were in a very bad place. I have no doubt that you would have taken your life in a moment of deep sorrow. You were done. You had made up your mind. It was just a matter of time."

"Does my mother know this? Does Jorge know this?"

"I don't really know. I don't think you would discuss too much of yourself with them."

I am afraid. I am afraid of the unknown. I am afraid of what I've left behind that I can't remember and the things I do remember. I have had horrible nightmares. Horrific scenes of violence.

I feel the nausea racing itself up to my throat. I stop concentrating on it to stay down.

I sit in silence. I stare at the swing set, the perfect manicured backyard, the picket fence, beautiful palm trees. I stare at a world known to me only in movies. I sit trying to find distance from what I know and what I don't know. I am trying to understand that this life is running parallel to my own. I can smell it. I can taste it. I can feel it, but I can't grab it. It seems to be slipping away from me. I want to stay. I cannot retain and process the suicide issue. It is not coming from me. It is external and doesn't mix with who I am right now. I console myself. My thoughts are wide open and then I open up to her.

"Did you know that Nathan and I had a violent relationship?"

"No, I didn't. You really never discussed your marriage."

"We did. At least we did in the beginning. I can only remember a little more than a year of our marriage. I wanted to make him into a responsible man. I was fighting with him constantly. I don't think it turned out too well. We got a divorce. I tossed and turned last night thinking about my father and how much Jorge reminds me of him physically. I thought about what it must feel like for these kids not to see their father. Nathan has two sons. He had criticized my father for not being there for me. History repeats itself."

I stare at the ground and continue while trying to place parts into their right place. "Jorge reminds me of what I have missed. I can't pinpoint the lack of trust. He reminds me of tension. He reminds me of insecurities. He reminds me of fear that I can't remember, but a little voice in me whispers to be aware of his words. He seems to be a nice man. Aside from the age difference there is more to our story that I can't comprehend right now."

"I know, I know." She holds me. She wraps her arms around me, letting me be me. She lets me open up and fly like a frightened butterfly. She allows me to let go. She's helping me let go.

"I don't know why I am telling you all this."

"Because there is a part of you that knows me! You call me your Spiritual Mama. I think you need to go back to the hospital to get your head checked on. I agree with Monique. These headaches are not normal. There is treatment for this. Do you want to go back?"

"Yes, if you take me. Yes."

"We can do that."

Convincing my mother and Jorge to take me back to the hospital isn't easy. Neither agrees with Monique. Ultimately it is up to me. I want to go back. I want to get better. I want to be out of this house from all these people. I need something strong for the pain. I need assurance that my memory will come back. I need what I can't find at this moment: hope.

About eighteen hours later I wake to a woman touching my hair. She pulls on it gently and then with a desire to take it off my scalp like a wig.

"You have such nice short hair." She's shaking as she tugs tightly on it.

I push the red button on the side of the wall and immediately sit up, telling her to please leave my room. I see the silhouette of an older woman staring at me with shock. She doesn't seem to comprehend what she's done wrong. A nurse comes in, tells her that she needs to go back to her room and escorts her out. I've been awakened every hour and a half to make sure I haven't swallowed my tongue or God knows what the living hell they are checking for: a pulse, a life, or just aggravating me enough to take the medicine they have tried to push down my throat to sedate me. I don't know.

I have been institutionalized. I am now officially in Hell. The woman on the bed next to me is crying. She's been crying all night long. Her wrists are wrapped, bandaged, contained. Her lifeforce seems to be inside those bandages and no amount of medicine has given her peace to sleep.

I hear screams from down the hall. I get up to use the bathroom. The lights blind me. There are no mirrors in this place. Every piece of furniture is nailed to the walls. I barely make it to the toilet before I vomit all of my liquid. I haven't had food. Hours prior to getting this priceless suite, down in the receiving area a homeless woman wanted to sit on me and force feed me.

"We don't take that fucking anorexia shit around here. I will sit on your fucking ass and force feed you."

I asked if she wanted my food. She had no problem feeding it to herself. The smells of rot and decay covered by the sterile scent of ammonia and cleaners kept me down on the bed. The sounds of incoherent conversations among four others waiting for rooms pricked and pulled at my headache. My body, now over the toilet, is mangled. The bruises on my arms are visible from all the needles in the hospital. The bumps on my head are tender and painful. My thoughts are pushing on them. Each sentence creates a tug that cannot attach to the next. I want to go home. I will never go back home. The home I remember is no longer available.

The doctor in the emergency room was an arrogant asshole. He asked about the severity of my pain. I looked at my friends, Monique and Lisa, "The pain is so much that I would jump off a bridge to end it."

Monique tries to explain to him about the leakage and he hears nothing. She explains that I need a patch to close the holes but the man puts his hands in the air and walks away. Several hours later I was "Baker Acted." I lost my rights to my own life. I awake to a handcuff on my left wrist and the bars of the bed. This is not surprising, as I have *never* had rights to my own life, but now a technical mistake lands me in a shit of a mental hospital. I later learn that the Baker Act in Florida is an involuntary institutionalization and examination where I can't say anything until I am examined by a psychiatrist. I asked for a simpler terminology since I don't understand how this mistake has happened. I keep throwing up and the woman in the room cries louder.

A nurse comes in. "What do you need?"

"My memory. My home. My life."

"Yeah, well I can't help you with that but I can give you something for the pain."

"Whatever. I need rest. Please don't keep waking me up."

"It's standard policy for the first twenty-four hours. We need to make sure you are alive."

Her words pierce through me. This isn't living. I am barely making it.

I wake to chanting from the hallway. The women and men are all on one floor separated by the nurse's station. I hear a woman scream, "He grabbed my tit! He's gonna fuck me!" For a second, I forget where I am. The medicine has drugged me but I am not in the tormented pain I was hours before. I have no concept of time.

I walk to the hall towards the nurses' station.

"Can I see the doctor today?"

"He will be in later." You need to go to the room down the hall and eat something.

I am drugged. I can feel my body operating in slow motion.

"I'm not hungry." I hold my head to the side. The pain is coming back. My back feels the prickling of pain all the way down the spine. It shoots down to my pelvic area.

"Miss, I don't belong here. This has been a huge mistake. I need to speak to someone to get out of here."

The nurses aren't fazed by anything I say. There are several patients walking in dazes and they all start chanting, "I don't belong here. I don't belong here. I don't belong here."

An Asian nurse steers me gently towards the gathering room. "You can't be starting this commotion here. You will be seen by the doctor whenever he gets here. Do not start this nonsense with the other patients."

I sit at a table. Pictures of the towers keep replaying on the television. September 11 has marked something in history. I have no clue what is happening, and the images run through me with sorrow. I cannot understand the scenes. I sit alone and put my head on the table. Breakfast is brought out. I push it to the other side.

"Hey, you! You gonna eat your eggs?" I hear the sound of a strong Spanish accent.

I look up and a woman in her fifties is standing there pointing at my eggs.

"You can have them."

She sits next to me. She starts to ask where I am from, why I am here, what happened to my head, why I have a giant bruise on my face. I hear her pitch but can't make out the rest of her words. I don't understand if I am dreaming. I want to go home. I am cold, broken, mangled, and disconnected.

"Hey, you. You listening to me? Did you get raped or some shit?"
She demands an answer.

I look up at her.

"Yeah, bitch, I'm talking to you. What's your deal? Why you
here?" She's relentless.

"Mistake! I'm here by mistake."

"Yeah, me too. Most of us are here by a mistake, two, three...
sometimes four." She laughs out loud. Others laugh and begin
chanting again, "I don't belong here...."

"Where you from, lady?" She continues and her hard tone moves
through the inside of my ears and out of my eyes with force.

"I can't talk now. Just eat the food." When I try to get up, she
holds my wrist and pulls me down again.

"Now, I'm gonna make it easy on you. I've been here a while
so I know how this fucking place works. You smart you listen to
me. What's your name?"

I don't answer.

"Holy shit, you got some bad skin. I can get rid of those wrinkles
and freckles. I can put acid on your face. That's what I do on the
outside. Give me your number and when I get out, I can come to
your house and put an acid mask on you."

"What did you do to get in here?" I ask just to stop her harassment.

"Ah, some fucked-up shit with my son. He said I was gonna kill
him. I was in the kitchen and the son of a bitch started on me. I was
cutting meat and looked up at him and pointed the knife. I wasn't
gonna kill him. He's all full of shit. He's all drama. Like you said,
this is a giant mistake. Now, when I get out of here, his *ass* is *grass*."

I get up. I find the strength to move quickly back to my room
while she inhales the food. I am alone. I lie on the bed. Tears begin
to fall to the sides of me. I can't remember anything about anything.
I can't recall waking up in the past on a cold cement floor. I think of
when they brought me to this place, my mother, her crying, and her

inability to do anything to reason with the faculty. I think of Jorge and his anger at the hospital for allowing my friends to screw me like this, even though it wasn't their fault. I think of Lisa's words about wanting to end my life. I think of Cinthya and her gentle wisdom and if she had been a dream, a hallucination, or some visitor from another place. I think and think and it hurts and it pokes into places of my brain that can't find answers.

My roommate enters and sits on the bed staring out the window next to her. The fog of glass and bars makes it difficult to distinguish what's out there.

"Are you okay?" I summon a question that has very little weight. She doesn't answer.

I turn over to face the wall, the red button, the carvings of life scraped on the white walls that haven't been cleaned or painted. I cover my body with the sheets and wish I were elsewhere without any point of reference. I don't know where I am supposed to be.

"I don't want to be here." Her voice breaks my thoughts.

I turn over. She's still staring out the window. I say nothing, but I feel her. I am her. I don't know her story, I don't know my own, but here we are in Hell waiting for answers. Do we go back or keep moving forward into the unknown? We stay in that silence for a while. I finally sleep. The dreams are as disturbing as real life. I don't know what's worse. I wake to another scream.

She is screaming and shaking violently against the wall behind her bed. I push the red button. A nurse and an orderly come in and restrain her. I turn over to stare at my own wall. I cannot be here. I don't belong in this place. I don't know where I belong but it's not in this cold floor of mental fragments and pain. Every person is wearing pain on the outside. I see and feel everything magnified. I think of the flight attendant leaving a while ago whose partner died in one of the planes hitting the towers. I think of how he wanted to join him in death. I stop myself from the thoughts that prick and poke me in places I am not open to reach right now.

I get up again. I walk with my head sideways since I can't hold it up straight. "Nurse, is the doctor in?"

"Honey, we don't know if he's coming in today. It's hit-and-miss around here. You might have to wait till tomorrow. There's only one doctor on staff here and we are on overload." The I-will-put-acid-in-your-face woman comes to me. "Yeah, this place is fucking shit. Don't hold your breath for the dot head of a doctor. His Indian ass comes in whenever he feels like it."

She catches the disgust written on my face and reaches over to touch the wrinkles around my eyes. Suddenly she pinches me and I slap her hand away. She leaves, laughing hysterically.

I stand there in the middle of a hallway as men and women pass me in slow motion. I have had only milk and juice. It all comes up. I fall to the ground. The orderly grabs me and puts me in a wheelchair nearby. A nurse comes and hands me a cup with pills and water.

"Here, this will make you feel better."

I sit for a while. I feel myself leaving my body in a dream state. I later wake in my bed. It's getting late. I see the light outside going down.

I go back to the nurse's station. "Is the doctor in?"

She points to an open room where a man is sitting behind a desk.

I go and knock on the door. I can barely stay standing.

"Yes?" He looks up at me.

"I need to see you about getting out of here. It's been a mistake and I don't think anyone but you can help me."

"What's your name?" He has a bunch of manila files on his desk and he starts to check for my name. "Ah, okay. I have just a few minutes. Come in and sit. What seems to be the mistake? What makes you believe you don't belong here?" But before I answer he is skimming through the notes in the file. He holds a finger up motioning me to give him a minute. "Says here you don't remember anything past 1987. You woke in a park…"

I hear the review of my current life.

"I don't know how I got to the park, sir. I don't know what happened to me. I was taken to the hospital and had a spinal tap. It's screwed up my body. I am in constant pain. After two days friends took me back to get re-examined and a young ass of an intern Baker Acted me for letting him know how much pain I was in. I asked to see a psychiatrist while I was in the hospital the first time. I asked to talk to someone. No one seems to care. I have been disregarded."

"I'm listening, Mildred." He is completely attentive and I can see in his eyes that he sees something different in my story. I am in a mental hospital. I am in a hellish psychiatric ward. I can imagine he must see the difference in my attempt to rationalize recent events.

"The problem is, Mildred…"

"Please call me Millie."

"Okay, Millie. The problem is that there's a backlog in the system. I am the only psychiatrist on board here. Even if I release you, it won't be until tomorrow or maybe the next day. You have to promise that you will follow up with a psychologist if and when I get you discharged. It says here that you should be getting your memory back shortly. It says that scans show no trauma. You also need to follow up with the neurologist in Hollywood."

"Yes, but when am I getting my memory?" I ask several more questions that he can't really answer. He agrees that I don't belong in here. I find it a miracle of sorts considering the ten minutes we spend together.

"That's not set in stone. I don't know. I will put in the papers for your release."

I stand and shake his hand. "Please, doctor, can you make it today?"

Three or four hours later I am released. My mother is downstairs waiting for me. She's crying. She's letting me know what a rough night she had.

"I didn't sleep at all. I am sick over this. The kids are very sad. Jorge is devastated. All this drama has caused us a lot of pain. You are doing this to us and it hurts."

I'm back in her car and her words go through and through. I stare at the scenery. I stare at the unknown. I remember this dance well.

"You are gonna have to try to put all efforts to stop this nonsense and get your memory back, Millie. You are a grown woman and you are acting like a child. If it wasn't for Olivia pulling strings you would still be in there...."

I put the seat back as far as I can and let her go at it. She's on a roll. No need to interrupt her at this point. I have left Hell. I don't know if heaven or hell will be waiting for me on the other side of town.

CHAPTER 15

I enter the house and the two older boys come running and hug me tightly. David is holding on to my waist. I touch him and pull him off gently.

"Mom, please don't go back to the hospital."

"I am not planning on it." I look at his sweet face. I notice for the first time that he has my eyes. I see my lips on him as well. The younger version of Nathan is now hugging me.

"Mom, please get your memory back soon. It's chaos around here. You are the tower of strength and we can't take all this craziness here."

"Oh, you don't know what crazy is. I just came from there. This is a piece of cake!"

They both laugh and I manage to force a smile. I also begin to understand that they feel like me, even though I can't comprehend it all.

"I am tired. I need a shower and a bed. I will try to get better soon, boys. I just need rest."

The drugs are still in my system. My stomach begins to growl. My mother hears it and starts to give me a rundown of what's available for dinner. I tell her a sandwich is fine but first I need to shower.

Jorge is standing by the kitchen. He is not happy. I can feel the tension between us start to escalate. Something is familiar in this, and my body begins to feel the intrusion of this rage. How can I live with this man? How am I living in this house? How is it that I've forgotten to break through my memories to gather answers?

"Jorge, Mami, I am going to take a shower."

"I can take you up." He comes to me and follows me up the stairs.

I walk in the room, then the bathroom, and he is behind me. "That stupid action with your friends was senseless. I hope you are happy with the outcome. You know you can't trust anyone. At the end of the day, you only have me—and your mother—for support."

I swallow hard. "It was a mistake. It wasn't their fault that got me institutionalized. It was the asshole in the ER."

"Well, if you hadn't gone back to the hospital, you wouldn't have landed in the crazy house."

"I am in a crazy house! I need a shower. You need to leave me alone for a bit."

"I will stay here in case you need me or fall down or vomit."

"NO! You will get out of the bathroom while I take a shower."

Fuming, he walks out and slams the door. I lock it behind him, then stand pressed against it, feeling my heart in my throat. I see my body reflected from the wall of mirrors. I go close it and touch my face. The woman who is not me mimics my motions. I begin to cry, and each tear leaves scarring as it comes up and out. I feel the sorrow, frustration, disgust, and the ache releasing with each wet spot trailing down my face. There's a reason I've forgotten everything. There's pain here.

I begin the shower, undressing my frail body held up by pain. I stand under the hot water, allowing it to slash out every second of the past few days. I want to go home. I want my memory back. I want my life back.

CHAPTER 16

I'm lying in bed when the flashes come. Flashes of me pregnant, then of Nate's birth. It is so surreal, the way the memories are inaccessible one minute and there for me the next. I remember the events that followed the birth. I remember the abuse from his father. I begin to recall pictures, events, dates, and endless emotions. I see myself as the main actor, simultaneously remembering these events and yet not remembering my life. Slowly, painfully, I start to put pieces together. My head hurts. My breathing speeds up. Jorge, who had been snoring loudly, wakes with a start and looks over the mountain of pillows between us.

"Do you need anything, Millie?"

I can't speak. I am nauseated by the intimate movies in my head.

"Do you need me to get you medicine?"

I gasp out a "Yes, please!"

He gets up and I can hear the little girl on the other side of the room moving erratically. I have no idea what time of night it is. I am sick. I get up quickly and make it to the toilet. Jorge finds me there and picks me up. "Here, drink this. You need to eat."

I swallow the medicine. I sit against the wall.

"I can remember things. They make no sense right now."

"Good. So, you remember me too, right?"

"You have got to stop and give me time—please! I don't know

how I ended up in that park so late at night. The doctor said that I would start to remember in chronological order. Please stop pressuring me—"

He stops me, "Millie, the drama that follows you! We need to get to work tomorrow. You need to see if you remember anything about the business. We will lose everything if you don't stop this charade. I can't do this alone. You manage all our finances. This is bullshit. It's time you snap out of this childish game."

I get up. This is not a life for anyone. For a moment I think of the mental hospital. I think of going back. Maybe they would help me deal with the rage that surges within me every time I am told that I am making this up. Like now, when the heat in my stomach is pushing up and I want to yell, "Get away from me, you moron!" but I don't. My head and body are trying to catch up with the demands. I get to bed and crash. I don't know anything at this point. I hear his words in a distant world. I can't make them out. I pass out.

The next morning the children are gone. They've been taken to wherever they go: different schools and daycares as I slowly try to make sense of their schedules. The nanny arrives, asking if I need anything. My mother returns with purse in hand. "We are going to your job. We are going to try and get your accounting work done."

Slowly, I dress and make it to the car. I sit in the back, with Jorge and Mami in the front. I feel like their child being taken to school. Things seem familiar. Nothing seems right. An hour later we are in an industrial area of Miami entering a place I can't pinpoint. Fear paralyzes me with each forcing of steps. I don't know how I will make it through this day.

I am taken to my office. I have no recollection of anything in there. There are pictures of kids, incense, candles, and a nice stereo system. There is a large computer and crap all over the place. What I presume is my desk is full of envelopes, paperwork, post-it notes. It is a mountain of work I cannot comprehend. I feel lightheaded in a way that keeps me from being present. Jorge orders a driver to get me coffee and breakfast from down the road.

I begin opening envelopes. My mother sits next to me, helping me make sense of what I'm seeing—mostly past-due bills show that we owe thousands of dollars to creditors. I don't understand it. Jorge wants to know the password for the computer. I don't even know how to turn it on. I don't know. *I don't know.* I am clueless on what to do.

I ask to be taken back to the house. I can't deal with the kaleidoscope of colors, sounds, and textures. The memories are returning slowly and I haven't yet gotten to the business part. Men walk in and out of my office—some are employees; others, customers. I don't recall a single one and my anxiety escalates. I ask my mother to make me an appointment with my therapist (I even know I have one, and remember her name is Charlie), but then I find her number in a Rolodex and leave a message. Five minutes later, when she calls back saying she can see me tomorrow, I feel a sense of relief and panic simultaneously strangling me. What's going to come up? What's going to come out? Why have I blocked this life? The questions run unfinished with answers. I don't know. I don't know anything. I am here but I am not.

Part 2
The Body

*"Our bodies were printed as blank pages
to be filled with the ink of our hearts."*
~ Michael Biondi ~

CHAPTER 17

I sit in the waiting room of the therapist's office. My mother drops me off and tells me she will see me in two hours. I am fortunate enough to get two sessions back-to-back. Charlie walks in and hugs me. I remember her and the countless hours of diving into the past. We enter her office. I sit down on the black leather sofa. She removes her shoes and gets comfortable in her chaise.

"How are you, Millie? I understand you've had some major traumas recently."

"Charlie, when was the last time I was here?"

She grabs her file and says about seven months.

"Why so long?"

She laughs and closes the file. "Oh, wow. You really have lost your memory way back there! You are my butterfly. You come in and out every so often. I don't think we've ever had more than two sessions at a time and then you disappear. When it starts to get too much for your psyche you stop coming. We do this, you and I. We've been doing it for a long time. I would expect nothing else." She doesn't say this in a negative or patronizing way. It's a matter of fact. I know myself and how emotions can start to suck me into a black hole. Before I allow them to do so I run.

"Millie, can we go to the last thing you remember of the night of this accident?"

"I can't. I have a blockage. Things are coming in order. The headaches are so intense that I can't force myself to think. I never got treated for the spinal tap. I ended up in a fucking mental hospital. I don't want to take any more painkillers. Charlie, they are eating away at my stomach! If one more person suggests that I am making this up, that this is a charade for attention, I will end up in prison. I don't understand their disregard for how I am feeling right now."

"I am glad you have that rage coming up. It's good to explore and talk about it. Would you be willing to allow me to hypnotize you?"

I think hard. I put my hands over my face. I pull my hair back. "Sure, let's do it. I need to get to the present moment. So many people seem to be counting on me, including these kids. Oh, my God, Charlie, do you know that I have six children?"

She laughs. "Yes, my dear! I do know. Okay, let's get started. Why don't you lie down, remove your shoes, and I will get a blanket for you."

We go through the initial relaxation techniques, breathing, and becoming present in this space.

"Millie, you are safe. If at any moment you cannot, or you will not move forward, you can return to the present moment."

My breathing becomes deep and shallow and I can see myself in my room watching television.

"I want you to continue with that night. What do you see?"

"I am alone on my bed. Gabriella is sleeping. Everyone has gone to bed. Jorge walks in and he is pissed off. He is drunk. He gets on the bed and accuses me of having an affair with an old man at our work. I laugh it off and tell him that he needs to take a shower and go to sleep. He is crazy, he is yelling, and I ask him to lower his voice. Eventually he gets into the shower and I am scared of his irrational behavior. While he's in there I get dressed in shorts, t-shirt, and flip flops. I go downstairs quietly and grab my wallet. I decide to go for a walk." I begin to cry,

"Millie, you are safe," Charlie reminds me gently. "What do you do once you are outside?"

"I move through the streets and end up at a park down the road. It's dark and there are not many people there. I find myself a seat by the lake in a pavilion. I am cold and crying. I want to end this life. I can't take the stress. We've lost everything. We need to move to our new home and have no money. Our business is in shambles and Jorge comes home drunk every night and takes it out on me. I ask God to take me. I ask Him, begging Him to just give me this break…."

"You are okay. You are just watching this," she interrupts as I cry. "Do you see other people there? Is the park empty? Do you know what time it is?"

"The park is about to close. Two teenagers playing tennis make it out of the tennis courts. Two other couples leave. I begin to walk towards the exit. I hear the kids behind me. I hear their rackets hitting the trashcans. Then I feel a racket on the back of my neck. I fall…."

I cannot continue. I cannot talk after this.

"Millie, it's okay. Do you see yourself?"

Through my sobs I gasp, "Yes, I am on the cold cement floor. The kids have run away. I am alone."

"How long are you on the ground?"

"I don't know. I begin to wake and feel the taste of blood in my mouth. I get up and look at my knees. They are covered in blood from the contact with rocks and the cement. I check for a watch. I don't have one. I touch my head and it hurts. There's blood on my brows. There's dirt on me. I search for my flip-flops that have fallen away. I begin to walk out of the park. Wait, I don't know the exit. Wait, I don't know the street. Wait…"

"Millie, you are just watching this right now. You are not experiencing this. Please breathe and tell me what you did after you found the exit."

"I…I…I don't' know where I am. I think about dinner and Nathan and how pissed off he will be if I am not there when he gets home."

I tell her the details of the walk and everything leading to the hospital.

"Now, I want you to take a deep breath. On the count of ten you will wake refreshed. One, two…"

In shock, I sit grabbing my chest. My head hurts and I feel drained. I watch Charlie compose herself.

"You've had quite an experience, my dear. How are you feeling?"

"How much time do we have?"

She checks her watch, "We still have an hour or so."

The memories pour in and they are not well accepted. I begin to cry, gasping for air, and cannot understand how I blocked all this out.

"What's going on inside of you, Millie? Can you express an emotion right now?"

"Ohhhh! I am so angry. I have been treated like a liar for a week. I have been treated like a drug addict for wanting medicine to help with this headache. I have been treated like a spoiled child. My family has discarded me. I have had no interaction with friends except my massage therapist and my friend who is a doctor. I have been insulted. I am so angry, Charlie. I am so deeply hurt that my mother and Jorge have not taken a single moment to listen to me, and now seeing what happened makes me angrier. I was out there late, alone, in some fucking park, because Jorge was drunk. I am thirty-three years old and feel like I am eighty. My life has been sucked out of me, just like that spinal tap, and I have allowed it. I cannot blame them for it. I have allowed this with all my lack of self-worth. Oh my God, what is this life?"

I am crying and each sob brings up an inexplicable ache. Charlie talks me through it as I hold my chest in my hands.

"Give me one good reason why I am here. Explain to me what makes me want to stay in this place."

"Millie, you are a strong woman."

"Charlie, please don't use a cliché. I know I am strong. I don't want to hear the psycho bullshit. I can't handle another moment of someone telling me to give it time. Do you know what I go home to? You come with me and examine the life I am living. What happened to my painting? What happened to prioritizing myself? What happened to the things I desired so long ago? It's all about children now. I get it. It's all about Jorge. And it's all about taking care of my mom who is now living with us. I will never know how I have allowed this to happen."

She pauses, and I become aware she has never seen me like this before. I have always been careful to be composed, even when releasing tears. The story doesn't end well for me. I know it. I can feel it. I have to put on a happy face, numbing through the events of fourteen years, and move on to take care of a home, a business, a man, my mother, and God only knows what else.

"This is not a life. I am just moving through the motions, pushing minutes into hours, into days and months and years."

"It is life. You have come to me for years with this song and dance. You have touched very little on your rape, your abuse from Nathan, the loss of your father, and the handling of mentally challenged children. You come in, you sit, you laugh, you unload short stories and anecdotes, but you have never let go of the anger as you have today."

"How can I not be angry? For fuck's sake, I ended up in a mental institution because I had pain. I ended up in a fucking hospital because I ran off to avoid a narcissist of a man who has embodied Fidel Castro and doesn't even know it. I live in a state of panic and confusion every day. Do you have any idea what that has done to me?"

"Actually, I do. You suffer from stomach ulcers. You have had breast issues for years. You have cysts in your ovaries and uterus.

You suffer from severe migraines. Your body has taken a beating because you have held onto everything all of your life. You don't release. You come in here and share stories. You don't share a life. You complain of body issues."

"Charlie, I don't know how to let go. I don't know how to release. I have been programmed to shut up and put out. Until when am I to do this? How long is too long? How do I let go? This small snippet of a week has shown me that I am disregarded. I have no friends. My family didn't even reach out. Do you know how sad it is that my mother has kept this to herself because of embarrassment, but when I am better, she will use it for drama and pity?"

I continue to share things that are new to her. I tell her about thoughts of suicide, ending it all and then feeling that my children would be scarred forever. They don't deserve this. I tell her that I am afraid of Jorge in ways I never knew until I had no memory of him. The memories are coming in, but some are gone and may be gone forever. I don't know what my truth is. Do I even have a truth? I don't know what perception is anymore. I don't know what real life is. I don't know anything at this very moment as I hold my thoughts together in front of a therapist without the fear of being institutionalized again. I am fearful of those things I never thought would happen. This is my life. I have no answers because the reality is much worse than not remembering.

"What do I do? How do I go through this?"

"Millie, I can prescribe antidepressants and we can continue therapy several times a week for some time. The medicine will help take the anxiety off so you can concentrate on getting to the core of these issues."

"No," I shake my head in anger, "I am not taking any more medicine. I can do this without the medicine. I have been numb for so long that I don't need more medicine to numb me more."

I sit while she begins to get her scheduling book out. We make a date for the end of the week. I have no idea what I am doing the rest of the time. I tell her I don't want to return to that job. She tells me that I don't have to and shouldn't let Jorge bulldoze me into it. I know better.

Walking outside to the parking lot, I feel the pull of my spine. Something is not right. My body is still in so much pain. I don't dare share this with anyone since I will not be returning to the hospital. I enter my mother's car, and she starts with the interrogation. Every question needs an answer but I refuse to share with her, saying only that my body aches, my head is throbbing, and I will need to return on Friday. She's not happy about this. She has things to do. I understand. I can understand the inconvenience of putting your own life on hold for someone else. I tell her I will find someone to bring me. She says I can drive myself and I explain that I am not driving until my body heals. I can barely see straight.

At this moment, sitting at an intersection with a red light above us, I begin to remember that night. I remember the feeling of sitting by the lake late at night and begging God. The light turns and my thoughts turn with it. They begin to travel as fast as the car, moving like a silent film in colors. I motion my mother to stop. She pulls into a gas station and I throw up outside the door. I want to tell her to please not take me back to the house. She has already expressed the need to finish packing because, "In less than a week and a half you close on the sale of this house and we must be out of there." I just want to lie down. And as the road widens ahead, lights turn. Stops come and go. I realize my life has little to do with me and more to do with everyone else around me. Everything is a journey into the unknown and the not knowing is full of fear and anxiety.

CHAPTER 18

On Friday I drive myself to see Charlie. I could not find anyone to take me. She is giving me two hours again. I am grateful for this time. It has been a challenging week of questions and very few answers. The children have their mother back home. My mother has her daughter back to care for things, pack, organize, and move through the responsibilities. Jorge has his mate back without mentioning what happened that night. Nothing has been discussed. It's as if nothing ever happened. I have not gone back to the office. I told him I needed a week off.

"How are you, Millie?"

"I am okay. The headaches have subsided somewhat. I feel like I can think, but in that space of thought and memories I get lost in why I have forgotten about my dreams, desires, passions, and self-love. My body has been used by strangers. I have had lovers in secret places that I have never shared with anyone. I have not been a good person at times. I have done everything I am supposed to do as a responsible human being, but I have also been selfish and careless and irresponsible in many ways without a single soul knowing it. Charlie, I can remember one-night stands after I left Nathan. I can recall events without specific faces. I went on a sex spree without any concern for my body. Who does that?"

"A twenty-something year old with a rebellious spirit trying to survive the oppression of a dictatorship. You've told me how Jorge demanded that you never date anyone but he was free to be married and date whomever. You did what you did in order to survive, and because of past traumas. Maturity doesn't even begin to truly hit us until our late twenties. The responsibilities of two young children and a home are a lot for a single woman at that age."

She has been seeing me for years and has never heard this story. I can see her face and the wheels turning.

"And why do you think you remember this now?"

"I must. I never had a normal upbringing. I went from Nathan to Jorge, a married man who for eight years made promises of divorcing but never left his wife. I don't blame her. She has probably been a victim in many ways to his dictatorship. He was an ass to her. He gave her a picture-perfect life without her having to go to work, but he cheated on her left and right. I knew this when I began with him. I am ashamed of that life. I took someone's husband. I lied to the world. What kind of woman does this?"

"A survivor. You did what you felt needed to be done to raise your two boys. You worked hard and put up with whatever came your way in order to give them safety and a place to call home. You worked your ass off to make sure Jorge's wife didn't have to work. You built a business with him so that everyone would be taken care of."

"I was a whore."

She pauses, taking a deep breath before carefully making a comment. There's silence in the room, and I can hear the clock ticking, my heart pounding against those words and the power they eradicate into the room.

"You are not a whore, nor have you ever been a whore. And you know how I feel about labels. It is healthy that you are allowing these memories to surface. I believe that once we get to the core of them you can release and move on. Whether or not it is with Jorge only you can decide."

"I look at him. I pity him. He has no clue of anything around him but work. Well, and this ranch home he has been building. He has zero knowledge of who I am, my dreams, what I need or want. He is cold and frigid until he gets to bed. He expects me to turn on like a light switch. I have been giving my body out for so long that I automatically do it without a thought. I can turn on and off in a second. How? Why?"

"Millie, you've mentioned the rape at eighteen in passing. You have shared the details but without any emotion or attachment. Your body was mangled and you were deeply traumatized, yet you moved through it as if it hadn't happened. You come to therapy to explore those feelings and release them and process them in order to heal. The mind can only do so much if you aren't willing to let go. Your body will take a beating. It will continue to remind you through headaches, cysts, tumors, ulcers, and heaven knows what else. Do you understand this?

"Yes, I do. I am aware of what I have hidden inside. I am aware of what I have chosen to erase and what I have chosen to remember. I had a dream last night about my dad. I remember how many times when I was a little girl my dad would disappear in Puerto Rico and call my mother in the middle of the night to meet him somewhere for money or whatever. He never wanted me to be there but she had no one to leave me with so I would hide in the back seat of the car. Each time I would hear his voice at the window I would jump up. I don't know why I dreamed this last night. I think I have chosen to forget so much of my childhood and its abandonment because it hurts. Everyone has a story! Mine is nothing spectacular."

"Yes, but it is *your* story. It is important to you. It is important for your well-being. Sure, we all have stories and shit that happens but these are the things that make us, break us, and force us to move through to another experience. Why even bother coming to therapy if you can't explore those things? Why just come to share story time of what happened to your son, or your daughter, and move through it with detachment?"

"God, I have been on autopilot for so long that I don't even know how to let go."

"Well, this is a start. You remember how you looked at your journal when you had no memory last week? You said that it was sad and you closed it. If you go back into your journals, I bet you can find more of yourself in your memories. Have you kept a journal for a long time?"

"Most of my life. But I know my mother has read through them and so has Jorge so I am not very open and truthful in them. I have little privacy anywhere. Do you know what that does to a person?"

"I can only imagine. I left my ex-husband because of something less than that. If you can't trust me then there's no reason to be with me."

I look at her, absorbing these words. She's never really shared her life with me and those words hold up a lot.

"Do you want to stay with Jorge?" she asks, "What do you want to do?"

"I'm afraid. I want a man to love me for me. I want him to treat me with kindness, and not just because he needs something. I was once so deeply in love with him, Charlie. I remember the day I met him. My marriage was falling apart. I'd had David just four months before. The day I met him I knew I would be with him. I fell hard for a man eighteen years older than me. I was twenty-two and he was just turning forty. I saw Richard Gere in him. I was 'pretty woman.' I saw a prince…." I stop as tears begin to fall without my acknowledgment. Charlie reaches to get me tissues. I take a deep breath.

"I loved him like I didn't know was even possible. He was charming, handsome, and attentive. He loved the way I fell for him, put him up on some pedestal. He insists that I have knocked him off that pedestal, and to be honest I did, years ago when he left his wife. You know what he said to me as he was moving in that first afternoon? He said, 'Don't think we are ever getting married. It's not happening.' Can you imagine hearing those words?

"I have had no respect for my body. I have had no respect for my dreams. I cannot talk to him. As my memory was coming back, I shared with him things I have done. He will never forgive me. A cheater never expects anyone to outdo him. He thinks he has always been the clever one. I am embarrassed and ashamed of my past. I have six kids. I have six little people pulling and tugging at me. Do you know why I have them?"

Charlie leans forward a bit. "Do tell."

"I had never put this together until a year ago, thanks to—of all people—the guy painting our house. He asked me why I had adopted all these kids, and when I said they needed a home he turned to me and said, 'I don't think so. I think you adopted them so you can be loved the way you deserve to be loved.' Then he said, 'You know Jorge…he isn't one to be faithful with anyone.' You see, he was Jorge's painter and had done his houses several times. He knew Jorge and his secrets. He knew his wife when they were married. At the time I resented the man's comment. I thought he had some nerve saying those things to me. But I thought hard and deeply about it, so much so that later that evening I asked Jorge if he thought I had adopted the kids because I felt a lack of love. Of course, he laughed and told me to stop the drama, but he also made a gesture of aggravation. Uncomfortable questions then took over the room. I knew when to shut up."

"Millie, do you recognize the courage it takes to admit these things? I want us to continue exploring this. Our time is almost over. Do you want to make another appointment?"

"I will call you next week."

She laughs. This is our dance and we are back to the beginning. I know this. She knows this. I know I won't be coming back for a while. She knows she won't hear from me for some time. This is fine. She and I hug and I leave lighter than I came in. I leave with an open heart. I feel the sun hitting my face. I feel the crisp November wind cooling me. And, as I enter my car, I know it will soon be erased.

Upon returning home I continue packing for our move. I go to the drawer of underwear and I find the journal. I open the book up. I cannot process what I see. Who is this woman? I start ripping it apart. I shred page by page, making a kaleidoscope of colored papers on the tile. I pull outfit after outfit of a woman I don't relate to in so many ways. It isn't the lack of memories. It's the memories I have chosen to forget and now cannot understand. I don't want to be this woman. I am angry. I am enraged by the lack of consideration. Things move chronologically without a moment to stop and address what has just happened to me. I am like this journal, a mere skeleton of a thick book left in my hands. Everything has been erased from a week ago, a month ago, years ago, and I can no longer live with the idea of my invisibility. This is not living. This is merely surviving day by day. The lack of purpose is overwhelming. How do I return to those dreams? How can I embrace the past without damaging the future? I will never fit again.

I move through the closet. Oversized garments get thrown in a trash bag. I will no longer be this woman. My mother comes in and questions my actions. I don't answer as I pull from hangers and drawers. She tells me to calm down. I am tired of calming down.

"Please leave my space," I yell. "Let me be alone! I cannot deal with any questions or opinions at this moment!"

"I thought that you were going to see if Charlie could help you deal with this craziness, not make you so angry. You should be happy. You have more than most people."

"Mami, please let me *be* for a little while. I am doing what you and Jorge want from me. We are closing on this house in a few days. I am cleaning out my closet."

She storms out hurt, angry; the pity party has begun. I cannot move on without moving out of my head. The memories aren't coming in, but they are there. The feelings are all wrapped up in responsibility. I have been told on several occasions that a breakdown is a luxury I cannot have right now. I have been told to snap out of this…whatever *this* is that they think I have created. I touch the back of my head as I feel the strains of something pushing back there. The knot from the racket hitting my head feels raw and tender. It is a reminder that I am not quite here yet. I may never be quite back. Three full bags later, I feel at ease with burying a woman I barely know right now. I am stuck between her and me. I am stuck between my mother and her. I am stuck between Jorge and her. I am stuck.

I see the reflection of the thirty-three-year-old on the mirror of the bathroom staring back without a smile. "I don't know you. I don't know why you allowed this to happen to your life."

Jorge arrives that afternoon, letting the kids know that they can start taking their things to the ranch. We will be making trips back and forth for days. They are excited. I don't want that house. I don't want this house either. I cannot find a home in between the bumps, bruises, scratches, and invisibility of living among others. Unlike the physical wounds, the brokenness in me is not healing. There's a deadness that is raw and incurable. I cannot mend it with the busyness of a job I hate, enormous houses, and the disarray of orders from two people whose lives revolve around them. I am lost. I am alone in this place. If I could put myself in a trash bag and ship myself off to another unknown location I would do it in a heartbeat.

My heart races as I mumble these words out loud in the closet. The room is cold on this November day, even for South Florida. I cannot warm what's been frozen for a lifetime. I feel the memories of Nathan rise up in my throat. I rush to vomit, missing the toilet by inches. There on the floor I see pieces of me, running through cracks of broken tiles. My head hurts from it all. How will I move through this loss? Where did I go? I recognize the lack of memories without the visions. Some things will remain gone forever. The neurologist expressed that concern. Given the trauma I'd sustained, he did not know if I would recover every part of myself.

In the meantime, I am moving through each day on autopilot, doing what is expected of me. Time has a way of mending even those things we choose never to remember. They exist forever in places that only the spirit can reach.

CHAPTER 19

We move completely to Jorge's sanctuary within days. I stand in the giant room that does not have a fireplace to separate the family room and the living room. The only thing I had asked for when redoing and enlarging the original house was a coral fireplace stay. I wanted to make sure it was there. Now trying to balance one giant room, the memories of that fight come in with a rush. I recall not checking in on the construction progress for over a week, then arriving one afternoon to find the fireplace completely gone. I begin to cry. A skylight remains where the opening to the fireplace once stood. I had not asked for anything else in this house. And, just as quickly as the memory rises, I am questioned about my tears.

"Why are you crying now, Millie?"

"I don't know, Jorge! I really wish we had kept the fireplace to separate these two rooms."

"Ay, Dios Mio!" He begins to curse in Spanish. "I think it's so stupid that you keep bringing this shit up. Be happy. Look, everyone is happy. Why do you make things so difficult? You don't need a fucking fireplace in South Florida. It's better this way!"

I move through the boxes in a snail motion. Things have little meaning. I cannot find my grounding or place in a house that may never find peace. I go to work, returning to take care of children, then go back and do it all again.

Our master bedroom is a place of disarray. We don't sleep on the same bed. It's been several months. As my memory was returning, I spoke of things that rattled him. I didn't know any better. Secrets have a way of coming out. I said too much of my emotions. We may never get past all that we both know of each other. But we live in a beautiful place. I should be happy. I am not. I am alone and I cannot make this right. The woman I was is not the woman I am now. The woman now is a stranger without self-respect.

There is still a significant bump on the lower part of my head. I don't know if it will remain forever, but while it sits pushing the inside-out I have also received the gift of artistic abilities. I had not painted in years. Getting whacked put something inside while removing the paralysis of picking up a paint brush. While unpacking boxes I find some old paint and brushes that I had not seen in years. I begin to doodle and paint old pieces of furniture. I paint the children's rooms. Each one has a theme that matches their personalities. I cannot get enough time to paint and get lost in a world of creation. While I am there nothing matters. I don't think of the lack of anything. I don't find the loss of my essence, but the passion I once had for creation. I am in God's arms with each brush stroke. I feel peaceful while in those moments, especially during the weekends.

Jorge is busy with his landscape and plants. The children have many acres to roam. I roam into part of my bedroom with pieces I get from the trash or garage sales. My mother keeps buying me paints so that I get lost in there rather than inside of my memories. We have no money. We are living off credit cards.

I begin to walk and lose weight. I cut my hair shorter and feel sassier than I have in years. Yet the woman staring back from mirrors is not me. I am not her. There are still hundreds of questions without answers. I remember a lot of things but there are just as many that I don't. I fake it when asked by the children. I fake the memories when asked by my mother. I fake a lot of things so that my apparent health and happiness balance out the lives of so many around me.

CHAPTER 20

In 2003 we visit friends in Central Florida. I begin to imagine my life three hours away from where I was raised. I can see the children living a better life. The business is still not as lucrative as it had been for such a long time. I sit with Jorge and express my desire to move. I believe that if I leave, he and I will be over. Or he may follow me, but something has to happen to jolt this relationship. We have been playing house but without really living. The stress from work, lack of money, my mother's presence in our home, and six children is unbearable at times. I have nights when I think of walking away from it all. I want to escape from this charade. I begin to dissect what part is the cause of the distress and realize I cannot move through the disappointments.

In the end, Jorge and I decide the move will be best for everyone. He will stay behind; my mother will live with Victoria. Once again, I am leaving my home, my life, everything I've known for so long. Though I have been through it before, I can't imagine how it will feel to be away from all that is familiar.

In September, with only $758 to my name, we go. As we drive out of the driveway, I believe the kiss I give Jorge will be my last. I embrace him with sweet sorrow. We've made new memories. We have grown together and, also apart. I am not the same woman I was before that accident. But there is still so much love for a man who has changed my life many times. Will he run to me? Will he ever see the woman that I truly am? Will he and I make amends for presenting fake versions of ourselves? My heart breaks in a way that pushes my chest and there is no expansion. The children cry. They wave goodbye to a home that's been ours for almost two years, to the only father they have ever known. I watch the house move further and further through the rearview mirror. My life seems like a dot when I make it to the end of the road. Things will either break completely or shatter to be glued back again stronger. Only time and perseverance can tell.

It's the end of 2007. I am cooking in the newly remodeled kitchen of a mansion in Orlando. I have lived in this beautiful home for almost four years. Our business was able to be salvaged through years of hard work. It had been the right decision for me to leave South Florida. I'd had to run away from my home/not home, and from Jorge. We are still technically "together." He comes up from Miami every weekend, trekking with him negativity, secrets, and at times folks he wishes to impress with the magnitude of our lives. To all outside viewers he has set me up in this castle on a hill and I am sitting pretty raising children. Most people have no clue that I still run the business from the confines of this home. I have become a prisoner of my own making. But time has a way of dealing with memories: those we keep and others we erase, consciously or not. I am still alone. Memories are there but I am alone.

The phone rings. It is my sister Victoria and she drops a bombshell: my mother's cancer has spread to her lungs. I stand there, still moving onions in the pan for the French onion soup I am making. I don't understand what she is saying. Yes, Mami had had cancer in her uterus, but she's had a hysterectomy and had been declared "clear" for several months. Now the doctors are saying something different. She has just returned from the doctor and the prognosis is not good. I am listening, I am still making my soup, and I still don't understand. I tell her this each time she adds another detail.

She continues to repeat the same message: Mami will die in a few months. I tell her that I will call her back later. When Jorge asks what's happening, I mumble, "Something about Mom having cancer again. I don't think that's right. God only knows what is really happening."

I keep on cooking, stirring the broth, seasoning the pot. I stand there in my beautiful new kitchen wondering what else I need to make before setting the table. Grief becomes a game between highs and lows, denial and acceptance. The sorrow hasn't hit me. It doesn't even begin to penetrate for days, weeks perhaps, and the affirmation that my elderly mother is not immortal. Each moment I spend inhabiting this body I am reminded that I cannot hold onto anything.

It has been six years since my life was erased. Things have been forgiven. Jorge and I have been playing a game for so long that we know each other's move before the other will even try it. I am happy during the week alone with kids, a huge house, and a business to run. But, as Friday approaches, my chest tightens, I have a bleeding, the stress engulfs every part of my spirit. I don't know how I can continue yet each day I do what I am supposed to do. In those six years, nothing has changed. If anything, I have allowed the numbness to guide me every day.

My mother spends her time preparing for death. Having been a master of hypochondria she has waited for and carefully anticipated this moment. She has always known she would die of something tragic. It was a given. Through countless hours spent on doctor visits, researching diseases, constantly divulging the ins and outs of other people's illnesses, she has been waiting for her turn.

In March, a few months after that call from Victoria, Mom comes to stay with us for a while. My sisters need a break from all that is happening. One morning, around 4:00 a.m., I wake to my mother's coughs echoing across the house. The sound goes through me like thunder on a stormy night, rattling the home's foundation, my foundation. I rush to my bedroom, where she is sleeping as the bed is much lower than the one in the guest room. I ask if there is anything I can do for her—she says to bring her something to drink and help her go to the bathroom. I do as I am told, half-asleep, half-awake, in a state of anxiety like I haven't felt in a long time. It's not unusual in her presence, especially when caring for her, to feel this solicitude. This is the way it is and always has been.

As I take her back to bed she stands straight and stops me. "You know I am dying?"

"Yes," I reply, staring at the floor.

"No, you don't know! I am dying. You don't seem to understand. I am a walking dead person who is ready to go."

"Yes. You mentioned it." I am still holding on to her arm that is much thinner than it used to be. Mami is petite—just four-foot-ten—but I have never seen her look this small.

She gets agitated since there is no more response from me as I continue to settle her into bed. "Do you know the sacrifices I have made to come here to be with you?

"Yes, Mami, I know and I appreciate it." I keep my voice low and as neutral as possible.

"Do you? I am here so you can see how I am dying." She stares mischievously.

"I know," I say, but she pushes me with her eyes as if doubting me. She wants to find regrets in this life and she wants me to join her in this party. I can see death on her; I can see she is leaving any moment and I want desperately to hang onto her. It's as if she's one of those balloons slowly making its way to the heavens. Eventually, I will have to let go—a fact she continually reminds me of.

"You know that I am very sick. I am dying."

"Yes, you have been for many years now." My response is like poison spilling out of me. I can feel the venom stinging me on the way out. It doesn't seem to have the same effect on Mami; she doesn't even flinch, just allows me to tuck her in with a forced smile and a kiss on her forehead. How many more times will I get this chance to feel her skin on my hands and lips?

I go back to the guest room on the other side of the house. I climb into the small bed and Jorge turns to hold me. Tears rush out and a deep sigh surprises me. I am not in a good place. I can feel that the next few hours will be a test of my character. The next few weeks include a final exam I might not pass with perfection. I start to pray in the silence of the room. He asks if I need anything and I nod. I can't speak. I just turn to my side and stare at the shadows of the room. I continue to ask God for forgiveness. I realize my mother is dying not so much from cancer as from self-pity, chronic dependency, and a controlling personality whose only security in life has been negative forces. I have known this all of my life. It is hard to feel compassion when the person is not compassionate. But she did the best she knew. She has loved to the fullness of her capacity. I have learned to come out of my shell in order to break the chains and try not to fall into the same patterns.

I call out in my prayers to Mother Teresa, as if to conjure up some of her abilities and tuck them deep in my heart. I am breaking. I want to find myself enlightened by humility and the humble surroundings of a perfect heart. Each sob comes with a struggle and a wish so that I can care for my mother, giving her peace on her last few days. I want her to say a proper goodbye to her grandchildren. I love her. If she were willing to meet me halfway without pity it would help me care for her.

Mami is ill because she wants to be. This thought comes out so harsh and full of anger. Two months ago, she had dementia and miraculously got cured when she was told by my sisters that she was going to be placed in a nursing home, after I told them she was faking it. She was. She could be extremely nasty and made us feel like horrible daughters at times. This has been forgotten in view of her new ailment. She does have cancer and she has really given up on everything, including self-respect. I look back, searching for a time when she did not WANT to be sick. She has been looking for cancer all her adult life, trying to play the victim, the martyr to the world. But now, seeing a cadaver barely breathing, my heart breaks with deep sorrow. I am mourning her before she even departs.

As she walked in this evening, I saw death hanging on each step, breathing down my neck as I helped her. I remember a statement by the late Catholicism expert John Cogley: "Tolerance implies a respect for another person, not because he is wrong or even because he is right, but because he is human."

I am trying. I am pulling from the bottom of the Universe. I continue to pray for light to come to my spirit. I want to be here and understand her need to make others see her as a victim, but I don't; I can't. I can't grasp her need to be dead before actually dying. I see her body language change in front of others and know that she wants that from me. I don't believe she will stay here longer than a week, I can bet on it, yet I can't indulge her poor-me attitude. And as the thoughts pour out, a part of me erases the past. I am humbled by future loss. This is a rough night. I can feel the hours lurking in the distance. The morning light will come up soon. I am alone in this loss.

CHAPTER 21

It's late in the afternoon. The kids have arrived from school to find her lying outside on the terrace bundled up in a ball. They don't know that their Momo is not going to make it too much longer. Sometime during the morning, she begs me to find someone to cure her. I tell her that the only person who can do this is herself. She needs to eat. She needs to put effort into walking. I made her a great soup with nutrients yesterday, but she doesn't want it. She wants to starve to death. I tell her that she needs to try just a little harder until her appetite can open up again. I get that who-the-hell-are-you-to-suggest-these-things look. She wants a medical doctor, more pills, more tests, and more awareness from the world that she is dying.

I want to sit with her and hold her hand and tell her that it is okay to have such fears. I want to assure her that peace is only a thought away. I want to love on her and tell her that she did a great job with me. I know she is proud of me, but I crave to hear it. I want her to know that I am proud of her as well for having raised us on her own, that she has been my example for so much in my life, but I restrain myself when I see her pity take on a new tone of disgust. I will give it time, I decide, then maybe we can share more than a glance and, "Are you okay, do you need anything?"

In my most shameful spirit, I spend a half hour this morning gathering strength. How this has become such a difficult issue is beyond me. I light incense in my office so that I can acquire my territory again. I watch the way my own body is caving through all of this. I feel an ache that moves through my own acceptance of life. I am losing my mother.

The next night, after some time tossing and turning, I win the battle for sleep. I wake around three a.m. and I meditate. I sit down in the darkness of my red living room, guided by the silhouettes. I repeat, "Peace, peace, peace," with every breath I inhale and I release to the world, "I am." I find myself in a garden. I keep breathing peace. I stare across a beautiful pond full of swans. I am at peace. I find a seat by the water and smile inwardly. I am peace, peace, peace. This meditation lasts about fifteen minutes. I feel new when I come out. I hear the new puppy crying, my mother coughing, the trucks passing outside, and it's not even four-thirty. Still sitting cross-legged, I realize that there is such terrible hunger for love in this world. We are famished for peace. I breathe in deeply and release, then begin to cry as I feel an overwhelming hurt and empathy for the woman whose life is diminishing. My mother is going to be gone from here and then what will happen to me? Who will I be without her constant expectations of me? She is dying. I am going to miss her.

I go to see her and tend to her lovingly. I want to start this day more positively than I did yesterday. Last night, as I helped her dress for bed, I had told her, "I love you more than you'll ever know, Mami." I want to pick up from there.

She had held my hand and said she loved me too. The haze over her eyes showed a different person. For a few seconds we were just two women holding on to that hunger of love, then it was quickly replaced by grief. I left her to go take my online class. I have made a promise that I will finish my bachelor's in psychology. I am pulling through it with the weight of others pulling down on me.

I go to her this morning and sit with her on the bed. I hold her hand. I tell her that I am here to help her. It's okay to feel these pains. It's okay to be afraid. She changes the conversation. I understand this is an unconscious reflex. I am okay with it. I also know she won't be staying here as long as I want her to because she misses my sister, Victoria, a bunch. They depend on one another in a dysfunctional manner. I won't go there. I respect their relationship. I am at peace.

By 5:38 that evening, she has not eaten a thing. I begged her at lunch time to eat the pumpkin flan I made her, which is her favorite. I begged quietly, while telling her how much I loved her. I negotiated until she got upset with me. Her body will shut down soon if nutrients don't start to come in. She is literally starving to death. I am reminded of the time when I lost my memory and how much everyone was on me about eating. I understand that it's hard to eat when you don't feel well.

I have prepared a wonderful meal, shrimp and crab gumbo. I want her to eat a few spoonsful. This is my plea today. I hold onto her like a cliffhanger grabs on to a rock for dear life. It is her eighty-third year—not long enough, but I know it will be her last. Periodically, I'm able to let it go and give thanks to God for having had her for forty years, but for the most part I just think it's unjust. I tell her with a smile as she awakes from her cat naps, "I love you, Mami. Let me fix you something to eat. What can I get you? Do you want to drink an Ensure?" So many of these similar questions get unanswered but her look seems to say it all. She has given up. Her body is going into shut-down mode. Her eyes are letting me know that, though her body still lives, her soul has already moved on.

CHAPTER 22

My mother dies in her bed, lying next to my sister, in the early morning of April 6, 2008. Just days earlier, I had brought her to Victoria's house and returned to Orlando, only to turn around and rush back after dreaming of seeing her tombstone with April 6 as the death date. I got to spend one more precious day with her, then Mami goes softly with the morphine, with our entire family gathered around, making jokes and loving on her while she peered up at us through her mask. She wasn't there, but she was still holding on to fragments of humanity. She needed these last moments of joy and reminiscing. She needed to know she has been loved to the fullest and appreciated for being the tower of strength for all of us. She has been the nucleus of so many key moments, and I don't know how the void she leaves will play out with my sisters.

When they come get her body she's wrapped up like a mummy. I stand in the room as she's being wheeled out on a stretcher, and for the first time it truly hits me: my mom is gone. She's gone to a place and I won't be seeing her anymore. I gasp for air as I see the white sheet covering her head. I cannot breathe. I have no means of sustaining my body. Jorge holds me. There's an incomprehensible and mystifying feel in the room. It's just her body. Her soul had left days before. I go outside and sit on steps. They wheel her out and I feel a loss like I've never felt before, not even when I lost my own life all those years ago. She's gone… for good. She's no longer here to manipulate, to tell me what needs to be done or provide lessons for me. She's no longer here to fall back and blame, to internalize my anger from the past, or to push myself to be better. I am embarrassed by this thought. I wipe my eyes and recall the ride here five days earlier.

Upon waking I had asked her if she wanted to return to her house. "Yes, please," she replied, "I need to be with your sisters." I packed up her things and made sure she was comfortable in the front seat. I put pillows around her fragile body. I gently asked her if she wanted anything else before we go. I silently watched as she said goodbye to all the kids, knowing that they won't see her anymore. By this point she was no longer in a place to truly show ego. She was there and gone at the same time. In her eyes, I was witnessing the veil of separation between life and death. There's beauty and mysticism in it but when it's a loved one it's difficult to swallow. It's a grief that arrives in waves of attachment and disillusion that can drown the soul. I stared at this shrunken version of a woman I have called "my home," thinking, *How will I ever move through this moment?*

As I drive down the Turnpike she reaches for my right arm. "What do you think happens when we die? Do you think there is a heaven and hell, like in the Bible?"

"I think you go to a place of peace. I think you finally get to rest from this life and all the lessons. If there's any hell it would be what we live on earth."

"I am afraid. I don't know what will happen to me."

"Mami, you will be better than ever. I promise. You will be in the arms of love and peace. You can watch over us then. You have done a lot in this life. You are ready. So please don't hang on if your soul is telling you that it wants to go. There is no need to fear because you've done all that you needed to do here with us. You've hurt. You've healed. You've loved. You've been the best version of you."

My mother smiles softly. She's there, but she's not herself. I keep driving, trying not to lose the tears or myself along the way. She sleeps on and off. I stare at her fragility and cannot understand how this is happening. I was against her getting radiation but my sisters encouraged her. I wanted to take her to a holistic doctor and she refused. Her health declined within months. Now, a silhouette of a body lies in pain next to me, drifting in an out of consciousness, through three and a half hours.

Two days later she calls everyone on the phone and gives them a gift: she tells them what she wants for them. My sisters are there listening. She calls Jorge and begs him not to let me go, no matter how much I want to. She tells him that I will most likely push him away. "That's who she is," she says to him. She had made it clear to me two weeks before that, "Under no condition am I to selfishly separate from this man who has taken such good care of me all these years." She makes me promise her that when she's gone, I won't also walk away from this life because "You will not make it on your own, Millie."

I never promise her that. I only promise to finish school, and to guide the kids down the right path. Two of them have finished high school. The other four will continue to move forward the best way possible. I will not manipulate their futures. I promise I will try and keep a relationship with my sisters. These promises are not enough for my mother, and she continues to press.

"Don't you dare leave Jorge. Listen to me. I have lived a long life." Her fears overwhelm her with the thought of my not surviving without him. I understand her struggle. I have erased the rest of the questions from years of suppressing that I can't make a life alone. Her issues have become mine. I promise nothing else. And in that silence, she mourns the loss of not being here to guide me through on her terms.

Jorge, however, does promise; he promises to take care of me and the children. I don't know why anyone lies to the dying. I will never understand. Promises are rarely kept.

CHAPTER 23

E leven days after her passing, I turn forty years old. I have invited everyone in the family and friends to my home. We celebrate not just the birthday, but my mother's life. That morning I wake expecting my mother's call, for her to wish me a happy birthday. Then I remember and the grief hits. I am struck by the finality of death. She was always the first to call on the holidays, special days, and events; now, I will never hear her wish me a happy birthday; I will never hear her say anything again. I will not receive another handwritten card expressing how special I am. On the other hand, she was also the first to convey the bad news, the traumas, and the negativity that would haunt my dreams sometimes. But she always made sure, to the best of her ability, that I knew she loved me. I will miss every single thing because it made her my mother. I love her. I will always love her. Now, standing in my library/office, I stare outside and think of the moment she passed. Did it go as I told her? Did she find peace? Will she be here with us tonight? Did she see my father and dance towards him?

Jorge tries his best to make the day pleasurable. We share subtle pleasantries—two perfect strangers occupying space each weekend. We play our roles well. We've broken up several times and returned with even less trust. Somehow the business always comes first, the children second, and so on. Part of me left with my mother on her journey into death. I know that my tower of strength must not crumble. I am to stay strong and be responsible. My body had gone through a hysterectomy the year before, difficult breast issues, and ongoing nausea that continues to wake me in the middle of night. I have lost my hair on more occasions than I care to remember. I have bled excessively out of my ass. I have had laryngitis from not speaking my truth, an ongoing cold that has turned into daily allergies for months, and insomnia. My blood pressure drops significantly when the stress takes over and I struggle to get out of bed. "Suck it up!" I hear the ghost reciting these words. I have no idea who this ghost is, but the voice is insistent that I push through it and move through life. I cannot sit too long or maybe I will vanish.

The rest of 2008 is a cloud of smog for me. I begin to notice that Jorge is cheating on me. This time, nothing is stopping me from investigating. My research on his whereabouts leaves me with physical exhaustion. I don't hear my mother tell me to put blinders on my eyes and keep moving forward. "Millie, that's what men do. You want to continue this life, you put up with it. He's a good man. You don't know how tough it is out there. Who's going to take care of you and these kids?" My answer was always the same: "I am!"

CHAPTER 24

January enters with a cold force, even in the center of Florida. One Wednesday morning at 3:30 a.m., I wake to the urge to go the bathroom. Reluctantly, I slip from my warm bed, do my thing, and approach the sink to wash my hands. That's when I collapse on the floor. I cannot move, I cannot speak, and tears follow with force. I think I am having a heart attack as my chest begins to tighten with each sob. Then, without sound, I proceed to have an intricate negotiation with my higher self. If this is going to be my last moment on earth I am going to beg and plead for a second chance, or a third. At this moment I feel like a cat with nine lives. How many chances has He given me? I'm willing to do anything to make sure these kids have a mom to care for them.

I cry for so many reasons as the pain begins to unfold and release me. I still cannot move my legs or arms or head. I just lie on the coldness in desperation as a deep sorrow unfolds in the silence of my master bath. The echoes of my tears can be heard through the floor back to my head. I want so badly to yell out to my children to help me get up, or get me to the nearest hospital. Instead of fighting the paralysis I go with it as a wave flows in the ocean. It is then that I realize my life is ending if I don't start making changes. I hear a voice from within me clearly say, "Millie, let it go and move on before you die. You don't have to suck it up." This is not the same voice that pushes and pulls at me during waking moments. This voice in my head is gentle, letting me know I am not alone. I will not die on this cold marble floor. Not tonight. I recognize the voice with a Caribbean accent. I immediately think of Cinthya back in that hospital years ago.

I know the voice does not come from the cosmos or a schizophrenic delusion. No, this is guidance letting me know that if I don't make changes I will definitely die. And with this thought I am finally able to get up from the floor. The wetness remains from the pool of tears. My legs feel numb and I am exhausted with fear. I am overcome with the reality that I'm alone. I can feel the panic of the unknown wash over me. Will I truly die if I don't make a decision to get a life of my own? I cannot recall anything of my wants or needs. At this moment everything is erased, and I feel the blankness of the night take me into its arms. I mentally return to the pavement in the park on that November night. I recall the same feeling of desperation. I do not want to die.

I have been completely lost in the mundane acts of taking care of everyone else. I realize at this moment that if I do not forgive myself, I cannot be a meaningful part of anyone's life. Forgiveness isn't about Jorge or my mother or Nathan or all my mistakes. Have I not been a good daughter? A decent mother? A loving mate? I begin to understand that I need to heal from abuse. It's been physical. It has been the emotional desecration of a lifetime. Blaming another is not freedom. I must take responsibility for partaking in these experiences. I have chosen them for the evolution of my higher self. I know this. The words move like poetry within.

At this very moment, I make a conscious decision to leave. Changes are not luxuries, but survival is. I sleep soundly as I haven't in a long time. When morning arrives, I can see hope peeking through the windows. I find grace standing in my room. And I find faith in a place I had not looked before…inside my own heart.

Part 3
The Spirit

"We must become so alone, so utterly alone,
that we withdraw into our innermost self.
It is a way of bitter suffering.
But then our solitude is overcome,
we are no longer alone,
for we find that our innermost self is the spirit,
that it is God, the indivisible.
And suddenly we find ourselves
in the midst of the world,
yet undisturbed by its multiplicity,
for our innermost soul we know ourselves
to be one with all being."
~ Hermann Hesse ~

CHAPTER 25

I sit in a beautiful waiting room of a therapist in Asheville, North Carolina. For the past year, I, along with my two youngest teenagers, have been living in the mountains with a friend. I left Jorge two months after the bathroom incident. I handed over the company to him. The business never quite fit in my life, even though it was making money. I had worked hard to make it part of my dreams, but it wasn't and could never be. Jorge never appreciated who I was; all he ever offered was a patronizing "thank you." Giving him the company was the only way to walk away from that old life.

My friend and I become inseparable. She helps me with the separation, pulling me up with each step. I help her up when her husband dies tragically at the age of thirty-eight. We are both looking for a path forward, and in the summer of 2010, we move to the outskirts of Asheville. We purchase a small motel together in hopes of turning it into a holistic retreat center.

After removing the material stressors from my life and returning to a simpler existence, I am forced to accept those things I had rejected for much of my life. By this, I mean the visitations from dead people. I feel like I am going crazy. I need a professional to take a look at me, allow me to share my story, and point me in the right direction. I don't want to end up in the loony bin again as I did years ago—one night had been more than enough. This requires that I be vulnerable with my history. I struggle with anxiety as I sit waiting for this woman to see me so my words can finally slip out into the open. I must be truthful. I am shaking in disbelief that I let friends talk me into this.

As I sit there, my mind drifts back over the past year. That winter, I had found myself in our mountaintop retreat—known to the locals as "The Bates Motel." While my kids were still trying to acclimate to the "poor life" after their previously privileged existence, I am staring down the ghosts of my many regrets. My friend/business partner is gone for weeks at a time—she has a job in the airline industry and we need her salary to pay for the bills. The business is dead and I don't know anyone in this town, yet I am busy with a constant stream of dead folks who come to visit. I am filled with a thousand "what if's" and I don't want to fail. I cannot fail. Each freezing day that passes I want to return to the old places of familiarity.

The winter is the worst seen in many years on these mountains. The pipes freeze and I am left without water for eight days. Two weeks prior to this ordeal the basement flooded, a monsoon of waterfalls coming through the walls. The house is mourning and so am I. I sit on the steps looking and listening to the cries. I call my friend while she's on a trip and cry. Every time she leaves our place something happens. I hang up and join the basement in this release. I don't know how much more I can take. Was moving here a mistake? What will my family think? I cannot return to the life I had in Florida. I cannot go anywhere without money. I feel cold and alone in a way I haven't felt in years. If stubbornness were a degree, I would have a PhD in it. I think this is what keeps me moving on autopilot at this time. What about living in these mountains keeps taking me to the unknown? How can I escape the visions I witness that no one else sees? How do I keep sane when things around me are pushing the insanity outward?

146

The days are gloom. My entire essence is going against this terrain. On the fifth day without water, I decide to go to the frozen pond in the property and grab a bucket of the excess trickling down the mountainside. It is two degrees outside. I am in my pajamas. My hair is up in a bun. I wear my water boots to help me navigate the path. I go down frozen steps, icy and slick just like the large pond before me. I stand on the ice waiting for the trickling to fill the bucket so I can flush toilets. I have a half-full bucket when I decide I am too cold. It's enough for one flushing. I make it up three steps when I hit an ice chunk and I tumble down the steps on my ass dumping the icy water on my legs. I am wet, cold, sore, and angry as hell. I yell to the heavens, "Is this all you fucking have? Really! What the fuck? Keep giving it to me and I will continue to take it. If I am not supposed to be here then show me a sign or fucking billboard so I can leave." The valley is quiet at five in the morning. The voice and harshness travels, echoing through the deadness of winter. I enter the house and cry on the floor in front of the fireplace.

I have no money to get someone to fix the broken pipes. They need to thaw and I need to as well. I am frozen in my emotions as I cannot figure anything out. I don't know exactly what I am supposed to do at this point. Every week is an obstacle. It's a challenge to make it through alone. I go downstairs to my basement bedroom where the water has frozen in places. Most of my shoes, including my favorite pair, had to be thrown out. I am spent, with no ability to think or find a positive outlet. The lack of sleep has added to my hallucinations.

These are the moments that bring me to my knees. I think of these mountains, the Appalachian Trail, the beauty and serenity of winter. I am traumatized by all the white stuff on the ground. I am not made for this cold. I cannot stay warm. I am afraid of the heaters being on too long and causing a fire. I am afraid of the gas fireplace leaking poisonous fumes while we sleep. I make sure the kids have warmth upstairs in their rooms but I have nothing downstairs in the dungeon. This dungeon keeps me awake with voices at night through its coldness and memories. I wrap myself in layers and wait for sun and warmth. It will be months before I feel heat on my shoulders. It will be years before I recognize the power of these lessons. In the meantime, I am stripped down to nothing. I wait for a sign and it doesn't arrive until I am ready to conquer my ego and self-worth issues.

The next morning it dawns on me that I have antiques I can sell. I have an engagement ring that I can pawn to buy food and fix the well and pipes. With everything in a box, I trek down the mountain, avoiding the black ice that has taught me to tread carefully. I go to an antique warehouse in Asheville. I enter with four bottles that are full of liquor and have a music box with a ballerina dancing inside the bottle. They are worth something. The Dutch company has been out of business for over thirty years. I know their worth. Two of the bottles get purchased.

I then ask if they buy jewelry, then immediately take the ring that Jorge had given me under false pretenses and place it on the counter. The woman checks the diamonds and asks what I want for it. I tell her that I don't know but to make me an offer.

She offers me two hundred dollars and I tell her I will take it. But then, as she starts to write the check, something magical happens. She closes her checkbook and tells me, "You know this ring is worth more than two hundred dollars, right?"

"Yes, I know." I stare into her eyes.

"I can't buy this from you at that price, ma'am." She hands me the ring and I place it in my pocket.

She looks at me and the remaining bottles, "You know God provides tests all the time. Some of us pass them and some of us fail. You have made me question my character. I almost failed another test from HIM. Do you understand this?"

I say to her, "Sweetheart, I am humbled by the fact that you didn't rip me off. The ring has no sentimental value for me. I would take the two hundred dollars if you care to buy it."

She says, "Thank God. I just cannot write the check. I cannot rip you off like that." Her eyes get glossy and she smiles in such a sympathetic way.

She asks, "What is the story behind the ring?"

I tell her it was given to me by my ex and it was to cover up his infidelities at that time. I couldn't wear the ring and had not worn in years. I want to tell her that it's okay. I am okay with letting it go. I want to eat something other than Ramen noodles, pay for my pipes to be fixed, and maybe take the kids to a movie. I want to buy water so I can wash dishes. I want to tell her, but I don't. Instead, I just say thank you for her honesty and turn to go.

As I am walking out of the store she says, "Miss, you are like that ballerina in the bottle. Don't ever underestimate yourself. You are stronger and more graceful than you can imagine."

I walk out with tears racing down my cheeks. I had not shared the story of the bottles and my childhood. I don't tell her that when I was six years old, in one of many Houdini acts, my father showed up with a similar bottle as a gift to my mother. I remember standing by the dining room table watching the ballerina dance inside the gold liquor while my parents argued in the kitchen. I wanted to be just like the ballerina: graceful, thin, beautiful, and oblivious to my surroundings. As I get in my car, I realize that I am finally that graceful little thing inside of a bottle dancing to a French melody. I have become the grace that carries me and pushes me towards the rhythm of God's tune. I know this. And forever I will be grateful to this stranger for pointing it out that I am stronger than I think. I am the embodiment of grace and forgiveness.

I now have some money. I stop for food and I return up the

mountain with a bucketful of hope, grace, and peace until the mountain bestows the next lesson upon me. It is not long in coming, and I once again cannot move through the mental paralysis.

Now I sit waiting to understand the other issues that have arisen from my solitude on a mountain. I don't know why I remember the frozen pipes. I don't know why I remember the ballerina. I don't know why I feel misplaced in this world. I want help, a quick fix, to assure me that I am not crazy.

A petite blond woman about my age comes out and introduces herself. Her name is Lorrie and she is a tiny ball of fire. I see energy spill over her before she even touches me. We sit in a gorgeous room. She introduces herself. I stop her and tell her that I've been through this before. Therapy is not new to me. I need fixing. I don't have all the time in the world. I can't believe I am back in front of someone having to share again parts of my life I thought had been addressed. I am not here to redo anything, or try to process the past. I need a quick fix for this particular issue. That's it. That's all. The lack of sleep has me on edge. It's in this edge that I find the discomfort engulfing me as a new person I don't like very much.

I tell her, "In order for you to understand what I see I must share how I see it. I am seeing spirits and things that aren't there...all over the place. I want to be tested for schizophrenia."

Lorrie looks me over while writing in her long yellow pad, "Have you been diagnosed with mental illness or any disorder?"

"No!" I laugh, recalling the one night in an insane asylum. "But, for a while now, I have been seeing things that I cannot explain. I am sure I am having some kind of a defragmentation or breakdown or psychotic episode due to a change of life. I've had extreme changes in the past year or so. These hallucinations are as real as I am seeing you. Now, living on a mountain away from others, I can see how the brain has formed shit to inconvenience me. It seems the past doesn't want erasing."

"How so? This is not a one-stop shop, Millie. I cannot just see you once and diagnose you. Why don't you start from the beginning? Tell me about your childhood—where are you from—and let me get an idea of who you are."

I get comfy in my red chair. I take a deep breath. My energy is all over the place. I can feel the panic coming on as I watch for shadows around the room. "I was born in Puerto Rico. My mother was alone at age forty-four with a little girl. My father was in and out of the story. For the first eight years of my life, we lived alone. As a little girl I spent a lot of time in solitude. I played well alone. Anyone who witnessed the time spent in my room thought I had an amazing imagination. I would speak to my Barbies and other dolls. I would spend hours speaking to my 'visitors.' These were grandparents and family members I had never met. They passed way before I was born, but they were in my room. I was never scared, though, except for one time. I was seven years old, and my father had returned for a few weeks. One night I woke to find my paternal grandmother on the stationary bicycle in front of my closet. I could see her riding it. I didn't know it was my grandmother because she had died before I was born. She told me that I wasn't dreaming. And just as fast as I focused my eyes she was standing at the foot of the bed. She knelt down and grabbed a casket from the bottom of my bed and showed me a dead man in it. Apparently, this was my father's dad. I was to give my father a message. I screamed and went to the kitchen to hug my father, who was getting water. I can still hear my screams. I can still hear my dead grandmother telling me not to be scared and that I would be seeing the dead a lot more. This was my life's lesson."

I stop with the story. Lorrie brings me a glass of water. "Please continue. Take it slow."

"Well, a few nights later, after my father left, I went to sleep with my mother. Standing at the doorway was my grandmother again.

I told my mother, who ran and turned on the lights. She asked me what the woman I was seeing looked like. I described her, then my mother got a box out of the closet with pictures of my father's family. I had never seen a photo of my grandmother before, but now I picked her out immediately. My mother did not know what to do with me. She begged me to stop the nonsense. She took me a few days later to my godmother, a well-known spiritualist on the island. I guess my mother wanted whatever was in me to be removed.

"My godmother took me to her little meditation room in the back of her house. Incense and candles burned and I sat my chubby body on a chair. She began to ask me gently what I had seen and how I was seeing it. I found these questions comforting. Someone was trying to understand me. At such a young age I had begun to understand that these souls could not be seen by anyone else. I told her I had been seeing these angels and people for a long time. After our little session, her advice to me was not to share with my mother. If I needed to speak to someone I could come after school to her house, which was right across the street, and share with her. But, at that very moment something in me began to break. I wasn't normal. The fear of not knowing what was wrong with me began to grow.

"Night after night I spent in agony, pretending they weren't there. I would see them and close my eyes tightly. My mother would tuck me in at night and tell me not to indulge in the nonsense. It wasn't real. I had a vivid imagination. When she left the room, I would turn on a nightlight. I had never needed light to sleep before. I also began to make wishes. I remember as if it were yesterday. I would take my little hand and make a wish on every finger of what I wanted to dream. I wanted Santa Claus and I would squeeze my pinky. I would go to the next finger and say the Easter Bunny, and so on. I would do this every night in hope that these prayers or wishes would be granted. Amazing what the fears of others can do to us, especially young children. My mother knew I was still communicating with someone at night. She took me to a psychologist and then a group of spiritual women who tried to exorcise the spirits out of me.

"Other than the nights I communicated with my grandmother, I have very little memory of the years between six and nine. I also recall the move from the island to Florida to be with my sister, who was divorcing. She and my niece, who was three years younger than me, came to live with us. I was no longer alone. I learned really quickly that my niece was afraid of everything, and because of this I never mentioned things to her."

Lorrie is writing the entire time I am recalling this story. I stop to get more water and get my heart rate back to normal. As I entered puberty, my anxieties grew. I believe that suppressing these visitations from spirits will cause panic attacks and disorders. I was an overachiever in school. I tried my hardest to move through high school with ease. I worked jobs after school and on weekends. I kept busy. I was happier being out of the house. By the time I began my freshman year of high school my sister had gotten remarried and moved almost an hour away. My mother took care of my grandparents and there was little peace at home. My mother was a wonderful woman, but her fears and insecurities were always lurking around every corner. Her overly protective ways suffocated me and at eighteen I left home and got married. Now, the irony of all this is that my mother had an amazing psychic ability. She was very metaphysical. She belonged to the Unity church, even worked there as a secretary for some time. I grew up learning about consciousness, psychic abilities, and the unknown. I don't understand why it was so hard for her to embrace my visions as a child. My mother was an incredible woman of tenacity, wisdom, and knowledge. She was able to read a person just by holding onto a piece of jewelry. Even with all her abilities she couldn't really embrace mine. So, I shut down while speaking very little to her about the things I saw. And when I did it was later, in her last few years. She had mellowed out with the uncertainty. I had several problems with my oldest adopted daughter and witchcraft. My mother was a tremendous help in making sense of these issues.

"Back when I was a child, though, these heavenly contributions of the other world haunted me and I had no outlet. I knew things about others I didn't want to know. Then, before I reached puberty, I stopped seeing spirits. I did not begin to see them again until I moved to the mountains a year ago. Suddenly I see dead people everywhere. They all have messages for loved ones. They all want and need to move on and expect me to be their messenger. I feel like the little kid in that movie. Each time I see them I think I am going crazy. A neighbor suggested I talk to you because I kept telling her I was becoming schizophrenic and/or having a mental breakdown."

"Millie, let me first express my sincere compassion to you and what you have had to endure. As for becoming a schizophrenic, that is highly unlikely at your age—most mental disorders are present before one's mid-twenties. Have you tried embracing these beautiful gifts?"

"Gifts? These are not gifts. Gifts, you can return. This is a way of living that is insane. I don't want to be mocked, ridiculed, or hated by others. I don't want to see dead people or any form of being that's not flesh and blood. I don't care to witness the many issues in strangers. I want to take care of our business, clean rooms, and not feel the leftover peeps lurking around. I also don't understand why people assume that I can allow this to come through all day long and miracles will begin to happen. I do have friends who are open to this. We have met people in this hippie town who are very accepting. But still! This is not something I want in my life…but I also don't want to take medicine. You understand?"

Lorrie takes a deep breath and reaches over to a small blue bottle. She begins to dab what smells like peppermint oil on her temples, then comes to the edge of her seat across from me. She seems slightly exasperated.

"Okay, so you don't think these are gifts? What would you call them?"

I pause as the words are about to come out. I had not realized how many roots needed to be pulled from me. The more I dug in, trying to remove these past traumas, the more weeds I found. I am appalled, sitting in front of this stranger and answering her questions. I feel as if I am bombarding her. In my avoidance of the external spiritual world, I have become very erratic in expressing myself. I sound as if I am on speed all the time. Lorrie, however, wants more.

"Can you tell me a little about how you got to Asheville?"

I share with her small details of my past life. I tell her quickly, running through a checklist of how and why I am here. I tell her about my six children. Some are still in my life. Some, not so much, as they turned out to be psychotic due to fetal alcohol syndrome and abandonment issues from a third world country.

Lorrie looks at me and can't understand how I am able to move so quickly through these stories. I have been spiritual all of my life, even when I wasn't aware, or acceptant, of it. I have been seeing those other realms in different forms—not necessarily ghost-like images, but intuitive pictures, smells, tastes and a knowing that came from somewhere beyond my psyche.

In order to live authentically, I needed to get to the core of why I felt such hatred towards my abilities. The damage by family and exes was deteriorating my spirit. I didn't want to be called crazy, satanic, demonic, witchy, psychotic, or the other many labels I heard along the way. I wanted to be accepted. I couldn't embrace what I was witnessing without questioning the analytical part of it all. I am the world's biggest skeptic. I tell her that skepticism is part of my DNA and it contradicts everything I am now witnessing. I cannot google the things I am seeing and find a rational reason for them.

We make another two-hour appointment for the following week.

I assure her that I won't be coming back after that. "You will fix me and I can stop seeing these suckers, right?" She walks me out of her place. I don't feel I am any closer to getting rid of my visions.

CHAPTER 26

One of the most amazing benefits of living on a mountain is being surrounded by nature. Having lived in cities all of my life, I had never experienced the freedom of inhaling and exhaling pure air. Months ago, I began to hike through nearby mountains. I got hooked on the feeling of being alone in the wilderness. It is the only place where I don't see or feel anything but myself. I feel closer to God. I feel the presence of life and the heavens. Living in an old motel, which once was a camp for troubled girls, I can feel imprints of negativity and desperation within its walls. I am not sleeping at night. I'd rather get lost in the woods.

In September, while returning to my car after a hike with a new friend, I fall on ice and slam—hard—into a metal fence. I hit it between my breasts, then I heard something pop and the air from my lungs became shallow. The fall literally knocked the air out of me. Hours later my friend is dragging me to the emergency room. After several x-rays I'm told that I had sprained my chest cavity and bruised my rib cage. I am to rest up for several weeks. No more hiking up the mountain twice a day—or doing anything else—to avoid the visions. What I resist will continue to persist. I was literally off my feet listening to everything around me. In that opening of my chest cavity, my heart was also opening to everything. I could hear colors, taste the world around me, and feel things that were magnified to the umpteenth degree.

"It took weeks to heal." I tell Lorrie in our next session. "I couldn't play outside. I was unable to do anything but sit—and without television or music. Something spiritual had cracked open in my chest."

"Explain this about hearing the colors, and about not being able to listen to music." She grabs ahold of her peppermint essential bottle and dabs wickedly on her temples. She massages her hands and moves to the edge of her seat, just as she had done during our first meeting.

"I don't know. I can't explain it. Anything with red, orange, or bright colors made me sick. I could only wear white. I had to change my bedding to white and be careful about the color of foods I was eating. Just sitting on this red chair would have been uncomfortable. I would be coming out of my skin. My cousin, who is an amazing healer, performed Reiki on me. She was able to adjust the energy around my auras and align my chakras. Everything has heightened but I can function within my space now."

I don't share the details of that night my cousin laid hands on me. I don't tell her how my body began to constrict and make strange movements, like arching my back off the floor completely. Still, just sharing this story, I can see what my rambunctious attitude does to Lorrie's spirit.

She writes. She gathers her thoughts. Her intuitive self understands this. Now her psychological and analytical brain begins to ask questions.

"What would make you feel at ease with these abilities? Have you ever tried hypnosis?"

"Yes." I sit thinking of the last time I had it done and how anger rose within seconds from witnessing a movie of injustice in my life. I tell her I would be willing to try it, but to please not take me to any past lives.

"We can go as far and deep as you allow. We have time, why don't we try it now?"

I follow her to a back room with a massage table. I slide on it, she covers me and, before I know it, I am going down the rabbit hole. I am sharing with her experiences I have forgotten since childhood. Every so often I cry and she guides me to calmness. I go deeper in consciousness, into a place of pure universal oneness. I speak of places and things I had not remembered...ever. I speak of truth, wisdom, and love from a higher plane of existence. It's the first time that guides/masters/divine wisdom has been allowed to come through, without being stopped by my ego. The messages are not demonic or insane. They are of love and my life's purpose. And through each word I am guided to accept this impartment of gifts bestowed in my path. I am in a place in between worlds. I watch a movie of my soul traveling back into the galaxy, and with each passing star I understand that my fear is not mine—it stems from my mother, family, strangers, past relationships, and those who cannot grasp the truth. There's no anxiety in this moment. There's no judgment or criticism. There's no bigotry. There's nothing but the ecstasy of calmness through divine love and acceptance.

It's difficult to return to a body when witnessing such tremendous freedom; however, as Lorrie counts backwards to one, I find the relaxation needed to proceed with these abilities. They have been provided to heal and help others. I can embrace the word "healer" rather than deny it and substitute it with something else. I can accept for a moment that I am to teach and help mankind. The imbalance is aligned and I feel the joy in this harmony. For at least several months, I am accepting of what I have witnessed in that other world that we deny in waking hours. I am made whole through this process. But unfortunately, it will take another death to open me completely to my truth.

I return to Lorrie several times. I begin to accept things as I see them. I share with my friends. I make new friends in the mountains who appreciate me. No one judges. We are all trying to find our way. Parts of me cannot let go of the past. Spiritual awakening requires presence and forgiveness of past traumas. I begin to make amends with all the obstacles, losses, and mistakes. I cannot change what I did back there. I cannot move through the next stage without accepting the aloneness and heartache I have discarded so easily by moving to the mountains. I came here as an escape. Being alone, especially during the winter when the business is slow, brings up regrets that I can't handle. With every layer of stripping the smell of disgust gets stronger. It's not easy to live among the living with one foot in the past.

Part 4
Love Transcends

"Love flies, runs, leaps for joy; it is free and unrestrained. Love gives all for all, resting in One who is highest above all things, from whom every good flows and proceeds. Love does not regard the gifts, but turns to the Giver of all good gifts. Love knows no limits, but ardently transcends all bounds. Love feels no burden, takes no account of toil, attempts things beyond its strength; love sees nothing as impossible, for it feels able to achieve all things. Love therefore does great things; it is strange and effective; while he who lacks love faints and fails."
~ Thomas à Kempis ~

CHAPTER 27

A pril is my birthday month, and I celebrate all thirty days. For the past few years, I do so by doing something different each of those days—taking an alternate back road I've never been on before, eating something new, learning an exotic word and using it all day, dressing in a different style, leaving anonymous notes for strangers to find on their cars that bring a smile; buying lunch for a homeless person, paying for people's coffee without meeting them, and so many simple gestures. I love my birthday month. So, after several attempts to find love again, I decide that for one of my days I will go on an internet dating site and meet someone. I wanted one date, one time, that's it, and then I would remove myself from the site.

On the very first day of making a witty straightforward profile, I meet Mark. We live an hour away from each other, so we choose a place in the middle, a quaint coffee shop in Black Mountain. We meet on a Friday. He doesn't drink coffee or tea, but I order a tea and we sit and talk for two hours. I realize this man cannot possibly be interested in my hippiness. His intelligence is over the top. At times I have no clue what he is saying or how it is relevant to the questions I am asking. He speaks of Star Wars and Star Trek, using nerdy terminology I cannot begin to decipher.

Back at home, I share this wonderful new birthday event with my best friend. Mark calls and asks to try "this date thing again." We agree to go hiking on Sunday, which leads to another date, and another. At the six-month mark, he moves into my home.

Our lives change completely. He brings his Great Dane and two cats and some baggage that I had not seen before this time. Amazing how things open up in one another once there is cohabitation. But he's been the first man who does not duplicate the many issues I had been dragging into past relationships. In this dance we have memorized the choreography to perfection. We are the most unlikely of characters to be united in a relationship. Because of this we love and respect one another, often pulling and learning about new universes close to the nerdy ones he already knows.

CHAPTER 28

O
n Wednesday, January 15, 2014, I wake feeling that an elephant is sitting on my chest. I can barely breathe. I recall the previous night and eating broccoli at a neighbor's house. I know better than to eat that vegetable. It never sits well on my stomach. I try to burp it out. I take a handful of antacid medicine but the pressure is constant. I massage my chest every few minutes. I go shower and recall that I am still healing from the hurt and betrayal of the previous week. My friend and I had gone to meet my new granddaughter in Central Florida. Born on New Year's Day, Rose came into this world with the odds stacked against her—namely, both parents are mentally challenged and abusive. The father kicked me out of the room on our second day, after I bathed the twelve-day-old baby for the first time. My daughter tells me that afternoon that she wants nothing to do with me because I am only interested in her baby. Now, days later, with such hurt and worry, I wake to this impossible pressure pushing from my insides.

Throughout the morning I keep holding my chest. Mark and I head out to lunch. In the midst of waiting on our food I feel a tingling in my left arm. He had been a corpsman in the Navy and could see the distress in me. My chest is no longer in pain, but the pressure is too much to handle and getting worse with each breath. He gets me to the car and drives to the nearest hospital. I tell him,

I beg him, to take me home.

"It's only indigestion."

I put my seat back. I've been here before. I am watching snow starting to fall. It is the fluffy soft snow that dreams are made of and I think to myself, *I am dying.* I don't say a word but I can feel my soul leaving in a way that's magical. Mark talks to me, asking questions, but in my struggle, I just want silence; I just want to watch the heavy snow fall outside. Each curve, light, bump is enhanced in my chest. As I stare at the snow, I add silently, *It's a good day to die.*

We arrive at the emergency room. I am checked in, vitals are taken, I am seated in a wheelchair to wait for a turn to be seen by a doctor. The pressure has subsided, but now I can't feel any part of the left side of my body.

I begin to think about the day before. I had a Celtic woman show up in my house with a giant sword. All day she stood in the living room. She had long-reddish hair and wore a green gown. This spirit never said anything to me. Somehow, I knew she was there to watch over me. Now I recall this memory as bloodwork is being done. The doctor orders a CAT scan, I am injected with dye, and the moment I am placed under the scan the Celtic woman shows up and says, "Mildred, this is going to hurt but we have to get you out of the way."

I am wheeled back to the ER and I leave my body. I am no longer in me. I am in a place of love, light, and infinite peace. There's no fear. There's just oneness. I am in a white room and I hear voices in the distance. My dead father shows up and tells me that I need to go back. I hug him and tell him I don't want to. It feels amazing here. I have no anxiety or fear. I only feel love. He tells me I have to return for the children. I want to keep walking towards the light and the beautiful sounds of souls waiting for me on the other side. Something pulls me back and I can't keep walking. In the distance I see Cinthya. I want to continue walking toward her.

My soul returns to my body. I open my eyes without knowing where I went. I don't know how much time has passed. My dear friend holds my hand. Mark whispers, "I love you, babe." I return to intensity. The ER doctor explains that stress is killing me. One minute my body is showing signs of a heart attack and another minute signs of a stroke, but neither has actually happened! There is no explanation for my soul leaving. I am reminded of things forgotten. Everything is a cycle. Things return to the beginning. This is a beginning.

A month passes. Within hours of falling asleep, I wake shaking, my heart racing to my throat. It is winter, yet I'm in a cold sweat. I am nauseated by dizziness, and the thought that I am alone. I touch the bed, stretching my arm to make sure Mark is next to me. Lying, staring into darkness, I realize the drugs are leaving my body. This is not real. It is the aftermath of poison in the body and every cell is in withdrawal. With antidepressants and sleeping pills gone, the nervous system struggles in shock trying to make sense of it all. Nightmares melt into dreams of characters and plots that make no sense. It is better to stay awake. I have this feeling that time somehow is suspended because I inhabit another realm at night.

CHAPTER 29

I t has taken four weeks to feel like I can be inside of me, like I can sit with myself in peace. I do not know if it's the efforts of integrating everything or the effects of the drugs leaving my body, but I have felt like I have one foot in this world and the rest of me is outside of it. It isn't the drugs, I come to realize. I am just adding more intensity by removing them cold turkey. The human body remains the same but the spiritual body is processing things quite differently.

I am not against medication. I believe medication along with therapy helps tremendously in getting to the many levels of deep-rooted issues. However, I know my own body and this doesn't feel right anymore. I do not feel a difference since the hospital. I don't know how I am supposed to feel so I remove the only Band-Aid that I feel is left. By doing so I begin to feel like me again—only it's a "me" I have never known before. I don't recommend this to anyone. I have a tendency to use the all-or-nothing method. I don't know how to feel. All of this is new to me now. The me before dying is no longer the me at this moment.

For decades, nighttime was an enemy. I would fall asleep early and toss and turn in the middle of the night, wrestling with fears, anxieties, and the unknown. But at this point, even with the symptoms of withdrawal, I don't go to the past or the future. I remain in the limbo of the moment, suspended by faith. This will pass.

I do not mention this to anyone. I don't feel like I am completely back from that other realm. It takes all of me to stay in my body. Mark has no idea of these feelings during those restless nights I am going through withdrawal. I can't verbalize these empty thoughts in the darkness. I spend hours staring outside at the winter landscape. I can hear the earth stretching. There is a nothingness in me. I catch my heavy breath and try desperately to calm it down, swallowing the nausea while trying to decipher what is in my stomach from this evening. I spend time doing Reiki, traveling up and down my body, giving light to every part of it. This goes on and on until I fall asleep, napping for minutes at a time. From time to time, I wrestle with my humanness.

Why am I even bothering with this?

By morning I am exhausted. I get up, open the blinds in the living room, and watch daylight break over the mountains. Mauve, blues, and oranges explode vividly on the days that I am most weak. That's the thing about being present: you begin to see the little signs from Divinity on the days you need it most. I also begin to feel heaviness for others close to me through distress. I am drawn to them through empathy.

For over a week I struggle with a heavy heart, thinking of a friend. On this particular morning I am at a loss. This dear friend committed suicide the night after we spoke. A beautiful soul with so much light and love moved on because her spirit was yearning to go home. When we spoke, I asked her to visit the next weekend for energy work. We made girl talk and spoke of being in nature. She was excited and told me she would let me know during the week. I had witnessed through her writing the past few months a downward spiral of hurt, faithless moments of pulling away, and agony for the unknown in this life. With pure desperation, she had tried to hang on, but it was too much. I was saddened by the news.

She and I had never met in person. She came here months prior while I was at a friend's wedding in San Francisco. Immediately she reached out on Facebook. We would send to each other personal messages of inspiration, and we discussed spirituality and life lessons. We would exchange sites on things that moved us to grow and expand our minds. At Christmas she sent me a beautiful book by Mark Nepo called *The Book of Awakening,* which I will cherish every day as I read the meditations. She was an extraordinary woman who got lost in the dark corners of her mind. But beneath the upbeat façade there was an underlying terror. This is why I reached out to her to visit soon. I feared the worst.

I, too, have been at that point of hopeless desperation, watching the ripple effect of decisions all turning to darkness. I know everything affects everything. My checking out could possibly result in terror of psychological disturbances for my children, family, and friends. It has been many years since I felt this hopelessness on my bathroom floor at 3 a.m. I understand the need to find peace and consolation. There are no easy answers.

Dying is not courageous. Living is courageous. The minute we take our first breath it is a journey towards death. It takes bravery, faith, and desire to remain here. Oftentimes our spirits have had enough. My friend knew this as she had also had a near-death experience several years earlier in a car accident. She understood the peace that happens once your soul lets go. She wasn't afraid of moving on. She was too exhausted to hang on. One of her last messages mentioned how she just didn't fit here anymore. I sent her a message of hope. She thanked me and told me to pray for her. My spirit somehow knew she was letting go, though my humanness couldn't really grasp it. Her honesty reminded me of some dead-end moments in my distant past. On the Sunday before she passed, she seemed better, hopeful, and faithful in her words of encouragement. I will never know what happened during the next twenty-four hours of her life. Her death awakened many from the coma of oblivion. It affected me greatly, as now I was questioning my life.

There are moments we look at our reflection and wonder if this is all there is. Where has youth gone? What will happen tomorrow? What's the purpose of this terrifying struggle? What is the meaning, the purpose, of my life? We have so many questions. Sometimes the questions are much more relevant than the answers. In questioning motifs, decisions, choices, past experiences, and the complexities of our stories, we reach a level of growth. There are moments we find clarity and moments when there is no light. Regardless of religious beliefs or spiritual practice, we are still humans. Doubts arise. The terror of living in continuous pain is too much to endure. In our own convictions we turn to God and believe that He will have mercy on us in whatever way we choose to exist here on earth or in the afterlife.

We will never know the answers to her desperation or reasons for taking her life. My only wish is that she finds the safety and warmth of Divine light as she returns to the place of Source. We cannot judge others for the decisions they make. She will be missed by many. Her soul is absolutely lovely. As I return to my prayers this morning, I hold her dearly in contemplation. *"To live in the hearts of others is never to die."*

CHAPTER 30

Since the near-death experience, dreams have become a form of travel. I enter places that seem familiar but I've never visited. They are not past memories since the visions are of modern times. There are similar characters of the people from this life, yet they are different. I ask the question, "Are we living parallel lives when we sleep, traveling through time and space as in a science fiction story?"

In waking moments, I experience synesthesia as I can smell things like colors (green is my favorite and I desire to spend as much time in it as possible), taste material objects such as the plastic from the television control, and hear things that aren't there. Just yesterday I went to the creek to collect rocks for landscaping and each rock had an intense vibration. I asked the river for permission and the ones that had no vibration I left in the water. It took me a lot longer to collect them now that I can feel the energy from them. Each sense has been magnified and oftentimes to the point that I breathe in and out to become present in what I am trying to do. After two months, living has become easier. I wouldn't want it any other way. The days have elongated and I have little regard for time.

The heightened state of consciousness that I brought back from that other realm really has no definition. I simply don't know what to do with it all. I am not a superhero. I can see colors around people, not in aura shape but through different parts of their bodies. I can hear their gestures and what they aren't saying. I can feel love beyond words and it takes all of me to refrain from overdoing it with others. I want to hug them, love on them tightly, and let them know that control has zero purpose. In the end there is love, easiness, and truth. That's all. We are asked to love, learn, laugh, and live. Such simple principles are lost on our human egos.

As I replay the sleep travels, I realize the similarities of this other Millie and laugh when I can. In some of these stories she (or I) has not learned a single thing about releasing and surrendering to Divinity. The chaos stalks this individual. I wake with the knowledge and awareness that at least I have conquered this realization now. In many dreams there is the question of deities, wisdom, and perception. In my life now I only know one truth: the Great Mystery resides in each of us. I saw IT. I visited with IT. I was engulfed, bathed, embraced in a light that doesn't live here on Earth. I was safe, fearless, without pain or discomfort. This Divine Energy exists in us and can be tapped into through prayer, meditation, and openness. I have returned to witness it in moments of solitude. I feel the light around me. I hear a silence that has little to do with our concept of "silence." The knowing is the virtue of faith and Divine knowledge. We are all washed inside of this enlightened experience.

During this time, I begin to have vivid dreams with Cinthya. The first time this happens I travel to her little Caribbean Island. She has a small shack by the water and the back of her house sits in a lush tropical setting. She invites me in and her embrace feels like coming home, only it is a home I've never experienced. She explains to me that she's my version of God. She tells me that I wasn't crazy in the hospital back in 2001. I cry. She holds me while I sob. She invites me to have my grandmother's delicious bread pudding. She explains that I can go see her anytime in meditation.

This awareness becomes a major shift in my life. Spirit has a magnificent way of teaching us about our purpose. We all have contracts of things to do and experience that we created before our incarnations, but that doesn't mean they are all going to be fun. In fact, they are often painful and exhausting. Truly, this human experience is not for sissies! That NDE taught me that fear is an illusion, and that the "gifts" from childhood were beautiful. I was also no longer able to escape my ability to be the best version of my spiritual self.

It is difficult to find your own way when you've been told and programmed from the world to be just one way. Finding your own voice requires courage. Testing boundaries, setting blockages for others to stop bulldozing, and being authentic to your heart's desire are painful. It is painful because of the aftereffects which vanish when others do not want to adhere to your truth. I don't know how else to live during this particular moment. "No!" is a complete sentence. Some will hear it and acknowledge it while others will continue to push through whatever suits them for their survival.

I will never be that other woman who feared life and didn't know it. As a wise doctor said to me in the hospital, "You don't know what you don't know until you do." After my awakening, heightened by the peace and hope of my humanity, I am no longer the lost woman I once was. I was rebooted. My memories are different. My conceptual knowledge is enhanced. And my heart has been opened to infinite discernment and love. I am learning to keep my mouth shut with what I see in others. If I am asked, I will share a tidbit. It isn't my place to change anyone's perception or life path. I am only responsible for me. As long as I find my own way...well, that's all I am here to do.

The God that has been taught through history is not the God of truth. There is no other God. One day I decided to research what the name Cinthya meant. It stands for "uncovering." I have been uncovering all the parts of me that needed recognition. The God I had been programmed to believe in is quite different from the one I experience daily. God is you. God is me. God is!

CHAPTER 31

April arrives with sweet sorrows. My daughter Tiffani has been beaten up by her boyfriend and ends up in the hospital. She asks to be picked up in Central Florida with her baby and returned to the mountains. Mark's mother, who lives in Central Florida, picks her up and keeps her safe until we arrive. We drive down and spend Easter weekend there. Upon returning home with daughter and baby, she decides she does not want to be here. We begin to notice the immense abuse towards the infant. Our hearts are on constant alert. There's a break in our household. We don't know what will happen through this. The two weeks that Tiffani is here are part of a hellish experiment. We are stunned, not surprised, but completely speechless.

We decide to take her to a shelter for abused women. They handle these difficult situations. Tiffani has been abused, but she's also an abuser. She is bipolar, has dissociative identity disorder, speech impairment, and other mental issues. She arrived at age nine from Romania. I was told she was borderline genius. She could barely speak.

We tried for years to get her operated on so she would not have children—impossible once she left home. The state doesn't agree with doing things without the person's consent. Tiffani knows her rights. Now, here she is with a baby, homeless, and wanting to return to the abuse in Florida.

While she is in the shelter, the Department of Social Services is called to investigate the abuse reported by other women. On May 28, 2014, I received a call from a social worker: I have only a couple of hours to go get my granddaughter or she will be put in foster care. My thoughts go all over the place. I look at Mark and ask for guidance. This is a man who has always wanted children. I couldn't give him this. I came into this relationship with an eighteen-year-old graduating from high school. The rest of my children are gone from home. I explained this to him on our second date. He was fine with this detail, but here we are, having to decide, at a moment's notice, whether to raise a baby as our own. I am devastated for my daughter. I am devastated for this baby. I am devastated for me. I know I will lose the independence I've worked so hard to acquire.

Two hours later Mark and I are signing for this baby who is sleeping in a car seat. I cry with joy. I cry with sadness. I cry for the unforeseen future. I don't know how or why I have ended up with another child. I joke, "Even without a uterus I still end up with a child. How's this possible?" But this child is pure love and light. She brings into our home a sense of peace, wonder, and love that has not been present in a long time. She is teaching us to be truly present. Even the months of no sleep, adjusting to little space in a small house, working the busy summertime in our motel/retreat center, and mourning for the loss of my daughter who is back in Florida and is not in communication, I am filled with gratitude.

My mind, body, and spirit have found balance since the imbalance of a lifetime. There are memories that will forever be gone, erased, and forgotten in places other than albums or journals. My body is still adjusting to the changes of a middle-aged woman feeling the transformation of the ages. I am giddy for the future. My spirit is the one who has evolved throughout the last several years. I no longer worry about what others think of my gifts, abilities, or lack of filtering for messages from "beyond." There's much to be expressed during this time as things are shifting quickly in me and I try to be ever so present, mindful of my lessons.

Love is the pivotal emotion that moves us. It transcends everything around us. I witnessed the Oneness of this love on the other side. I opened a channel to the depth and connection of others. I am allowing the Divine consciousness to partake in the human connection. It is through this portal of love that I have chosen to live authentically. My words, actions, and the way I move through life are examples for my children, family, and friends. As I write the end of this story, I cannot find a stopping ground. I cannot find a point of reference to sit and finish this love journey of mine with others.

It is the winter solstice today. My oldest son arrived last night from New York City to spend the holidays. The night before I found a baby book in a box and I thought it would be a wonderful gift for Christmas. He is sentimental like his mom. Inside of this box there were eight letters written from the moment I found out I was pregnant with him until he was born. Each letter revealed a nineteen-year-old woman's life and events during those months. The very first letter I wrote to this future baby was dated November 7, 1987. I didn't think anything of it. I wrapped the letters and the book and placed it on his bed so he'd find it when he went to sleep.

Early this morning, on the longest night of the year, I was awakened by a gentle female Caribbean voice, "Now you know why! You have the ending to your story." I was so exhausted that I didn't make sense of what was said. I couldn't. I went back to sleep but a few hours later, while changing and feeding our baby, I did get it. It's been thirteen years since my head injury. The date I got hit on the head was the exact date that I found out I was pregnant in 1987. It was the exact date that my life would change forever. All I ever wanted was to be a mom. I wanted ten kids. I wanted to be a professional, independent woman, but I wanted to be the most amazing mom as well. That day I thought I had a chance…even though I had lost another pregnancy, this one would be carried to full term. That date in November of 1987 I knew my life would forever change in ways I couldn't understand. The reason I got stuck in October of 1987 when I woke in the park was that I had just gotten pregnant. Now, you can ask, how does the brain do that? Why did I know exactly where to go back to? Oh, the intricate and mysterious part of our consciousness is priceless. I have been given the missing piece, finally, of why I was stuck in that date. I was given an opportunity to travel and make amends. I was provided with guidance, support, and the awareness that I cannot blame another for my circumstances when I am consciously picking those lessons.

Reading those letters of excitement to an unborn child has been pure heaven. I am grateful. This holiday season has allowed me to reminisce, forgive, let go, transcend, and move through timelines. I have the end of a story with a beginning of a new life.

EPILOGUE

In March of 2018, I was awakened at 4:30 a.m. by the spirit of my father. He stood on the side of my bed. "Mija, your grandson is in custody. Find him. You need to help him."

Tiffani had birthed another child back on April 6, 2017, my mother's death anniversary. I had called social services in Florida many times to see if they could remove the child from her care. They did nothing. Now, at this insane hour of the morning I text her, "When was Evan removed from you?"

She immediately and surprisingly responded: "February 14th – Valentine's Day.

That August, after six months of bureaucratic red tape, Evan was released into our care. Rose was so happy to have a baby brother! The family who fostered him are the most incredibly special souls. They have taken other children birthed by my daughter.

I remember that young child who believed she would have ten children. I have clearly come close to that number. At fifty-four years old, I am done. Then again, the Universe has shown me never to say never.

My life has been blessed by mysticism, surprises, and the sacred journey that is love. From the darkness of the past to clarity of the present, I continue to take every step with awe-stricken awareness that love is the reason we are here.

Lessons from Dying

Death is a taboo. No one wants to discuss it or face it because the fear of it is greater than the reality. I remember reading an article years ago that thousands of people were asked what their biggest fear was and they said "Death: mine or someone near to me." We have been taught to fear. But death is an illusion and only a transition.

Lesson 1: The hardest part of dying is waking up. I traveled to a beautiful place. The light that embraced me felt like nothing here on earth. Why would anyone want to return, huh? I asked that question for a month and a half. We return from that experience just because we must (it doesn't help that someone is pulling your butt away from the light either). There's no great mystery to it. There are moments in my days that seem to stop me for a bit and I return to that place of safety, love, and omnipotence. In waking up there is the melting of illusion. Life is a magical experience. Yet most people take it for granted becoming bogged down with the control, anxiety, and fear of living the lengths and widths of such gifts.

Lesson 2: Your body is a great wardrobe. Every morning, for months after my NDE, I had to resize myself to fit into this skin. I woke with such immensity. That was a huge issue when I returned from the "beyond." I didn't fit into my body. There was this expansion and greatness that didn't modify to what I knew was Millie's body. I looked around me and saw everyone's light so much larger than their costume. I kept asking myself, "How do I get inside and stay in there?" I stopped trying. I just went with it. Your body is the best outfit you will ever have. Treat it with kindness and love. Give it the consideration it deserves. Your heart beats to keep you alive along with every organ in that outfit. Love it!

Lesson 3: Growth is marvelous; stagnation sucks; laughter is the teacher of all. This doesn't read like a lesson—maybe that's why it is one of my favorites. I no longer see the problem: I see the potential to the story, the event, the issue, and the whatever. I see the drama behind the words when someone is sharing with me the woes and stagnation. And then I witness that turning those situations around and noticing the ridiculous insanity to them creates laughter. Growth is a conscious effort to move beyond what is not real. We all have the capacity to move past what doesn't serve us, or causes us hurt. Nothing is easy. If it was then we would not learn from it at all. Let joy be your travel agent through these stories you keep reliving.

Lesson 4: Love is the source. It is the only source of the Universe. It is the only source of your being. Love is all. You want love? Look in the mirror. It starts with you. Forgive others. What they think of you is their own problem and a reflection of their own insecurities. You are the beginning and end of all.

Lesson 5: Live now. Don't wait for the children to leave home, the parents to pass on, the retirement check to start rolling in, and the won'ts and can'ts that make absolutely no sense to the present moment. Live for today! Make a gratitude journal. Walk outside for five minutes. Be alone. Be with people. Laugh at yourself at least one time every hour. Look at the sky and its infinite wonders. Look at yourself and your greatness. Live every moment with awareness that you are on borrowed time. You know that feeling when you go on vacation and everything is just perfectly special? The moments are full of joy and just being away from your normal life is soothing? Well, that's your privilege for living. Make your life a vacation. Even in vacations there's work to be done, but you don't mind it, right? Play! Pick a childlike moment and return to it. Life is what you make of it.

I would be lying if I said that my life is peachy ALL the TIME. I still ride the emotional roller-coaster of struggles and disappointments that then dip into man-made stories of doubt. If everything were enlightening all the time I wouldn't stop and learn anything. The difference now is that I understand why those lessons appear in my path. I also desire to grasp and incorporate everything into the wholeness of me. I am grateful for visiting with deep emotions: anger, sorrow, joy, forgiveness, compassion, and love (to name a few). I believed in mysticism before dying. Now I live it every day. You go do the same!!!

Millie America

ABOUT THE AUTHOR

Millie America is a sought-after gifted medium and psychic whose readings and counseling sessions help others unlock their spiritual gifts and find their authenticity. She is the founder of Sacred Journey Inward, a daily blog and social media phenomenon where she has a dedicated and growing number of followers of her compelling stories. A metaphysical facilitator, intuitive empath, and cheerleader of love, she helps people find what is lost and remember what was. She is an Amazon best-selling author for her collaboration in *U Empath You,* an anthology and guidebook for empaths. A passionate storyteller and speaker, with experience in social work, Millie is driven to help others fulfill their potential and purpose. The mother of eight children, Millie lives in the magical mountains of Western North Carolina.

Connect with Millie:
Website: sacredjourneyinward.com
Blog: momentswithmillie.me
Facebook: facebook.com/millie.sacredjourney
Facebook business: facebook.com/sacredjourneyinward
Facebook group: facebook.com/groups/942663052799347
Instagram: instagram.com/sacredjourneyinward

Made in United States
North Haven, CT
27 January 2023

31733177R00114